THE WORKING LIFE

A
Mountain Man
of the American
Frontier

THE WORKING LIFE

A
Mountain Man
of the American
Frontier

TITLES IN THE WORKING LIFE SERIES INCLUDE:

An Actor on the Elizabethan Stage

The Cavalry During the Civil War

A Civil War Doctor

A Colonial Craftsman

A Medieval Knight

A Medieval Merchant

A Medieval Monk

A Renaissance Painter's Studio

A Roman Gladiator

A Roman Senator

A Samurai Warrior

A Sweatshop During the Industrial Revolution

A Worker on the Transcontinental Railroad

THE WORKING LIFE

A Mountain Man of the American Frontier

MICHAEL V. USCHAN

LUCENT BOOKS

An imprint of Thomson Gale, a part of The Thomson Corporation

THOMSON

™

GALE

Detroit • New York • San Francisco • San Diego • New Haven, Conn. • Waterville, Maine • London • Munich

"Happy Trails!" to Justin, Brady, Joey and Gracie Kuta

LIBRARY OF CONGRESS CATALOGING-IN-PUBLICATION DATA

Uschan, Michael V., 1948–
  A mountain man of the American frontier / by Michael V. Uschan.
    p. cm. — (Working life)
  Includes bibliographical references and index.
  ISBN 1-59018-582-X (hard cover : alk. paper)
    1. Pioneers—West (U.S.)—History—19th century—Juvenile literature. 2. Trappers—West (U.S.)—History—19th century—Juvenile literature. 3. Pioneers—West (U.S.)—Biography—Juvenile literature. 4. Trappers—West (U.S.)—Biography—Juvenile literature. 5. Frontier and pioneer life—West (U.S.)—Juvenile literature. 6. Fur trade—West (U.S.)—History—19th century—Juvenile literature. 7. West (U.S.)—History—19th century—Juvenile literature. 8. Rocky Mountains—History—19th century—Juvenile literature. I. Title. II. Series: Working life series.
  F592.U83 2005
  978'.02—dc22
                                                    2005005426

Printed in the United States of America

CONTENTS

FOREWORD

"The strongest bond of human sympathy outside the family relations should be one uniting all working people of all nations and tongues and kindreds."
Abraham Lincoln, 1864

Work is a common activity in which almost all people engage. It is probably the most universal of human experiences. As Henry Ford, inventor of the Model T said, "There will never be a system invented which will do away with the necessity of work." For many people, work takes up most of their day. They spend more time with their coworkers than with family and friends. And the common goals people pursue on the job may be among the first thoughts that they have in the morning, and the last that they may have at night.

While the idea of work is universal, the way it is done and who performs it vary considerably throughout history. The story of work is inextricably tied to the history of technology, the history of culture, and the history of gender and race. When the typewriter was invented, for example, it was considered the exclusive domain of men who worked as secretaries. As women workers became more accepted, the secretarial role was gradually filled by women. Finally, with the invention of the computer, the modern secretary spends little time actually typing correspondence. Files are delivered via computer, and more time is spent on other tasks than the manual typing of correspondence and business.

This is just one example of how work brings together technology, gender, and culture. Another example is the American plantation slave. The harvesting of cotton was initially so cumbersome and time consuming that even with slaves its profitability was doubtful. With the invention of the cotton gin, however, efficiency improved, and slavery became a viable agricultural tool. It also became a southern tradition and institution, enough that the South was willing to go to war to preserve it.

The books in Lucent's Working Life series strive to show the intermingling of work, and its reflection in culture, technology, race, and gender. Indeed, history viewed through the perspective of the average worker is both enlightening and fascinating. Take the history of the typewriter, mentioned above. Readers today have access to more technology than any of their historical counterparts, and, in fact, though they would find the typewriter's keyboard familiar, they would find using it a bore. Finding out that people spent their days sitting over that machine (with no talk of carpal tunnel syndrome!) and were valued if they made no typing errors because corrections were cumbersome to make and, in some legal professions, made documents invalid, is an interesting story that involves many different aspects of history.

The desire to work is almost innate. As German socialist Ferdinand Lassalle said in the 1850s, "Workingmen we all are so far as we have the desire to make ourselves useful to human society in any way whatever." Yet each historical period offers a million different stories of the history of each job and how it was performed. And that history is the history of human society.

Each book in the Working Life series strives to tell the tale of these anonymous workers. Primary source quotes offer veracity and immediacy to each volume, letting the workers themselves tell their stories. In addition, thorough bibliographies tell students where they can find out more information, and complete indexes allow for easy perusal of the text. While students learn about the work of years gone by, they gain empathy for those who toil and, perhaps, a universal pride in taking up the work that will someday be theirs.

INTRODUCTION

MOUNTAIN MEN HELPED CREATE THE UNITED STATES

Jedediah Smith was twenty-three years old in 1822 when he first journeyed into the Rocky Mountains to trap beaver. In less than a decade before he was killed in a battle with Comanche Indians, Smith became one of the most famous Mountain Men. Smith not only made thousands of dollars trapping beaver but explored vast new areas of the West. In the journal he wrote in almost daily, even while traveling through the wild new country he was seeing for the first time, Smith, a year before his death, expressed satisfaction at having accomplished every goal he had when he decided to become a trapper. Claimed Smith:

> I started into the mountains with the determination of becoming a first-rate hunter, of making myself thoroughly acquainted with the character and habits of the

Indians, of tracing out the sources of the Columbia River, and following it to its mouth; and of making the whole profitable to me, and I have perfectly succeeded.[1]

As a successful trapper, Smith sent thousands of beaver pelts back to St. Louis, Missouri, the commercial center for the Rocky Mountain fur trade. His greatest accomplishments, however, were to discover new routes Americans would use to settle areas that would become the modern-day states of California, Oregon, and Washington. In 1824 Smith re-discovered South Pass, which had first been located in 1812 but had remained unknown to most Mountain Men. South Pass was the broad, low gap in the Rocky Mountains that became the path that hundreds of thousands of pioneers in wagons used to make their way west across the massive mountains. Two years later, Smith led an expedition westward from Great Salt Lake to California, then a Mexican possession.

The trails and mountain passes that Smith and other Mountain Men located while searching for rich new areas to trap beaver were important in U.S. history. Those routes enabled Americans to expand the nation's boundaries across an entire continent.

THE MOUNTAIN MEN

Although author Washington Irving is best known for classic works of fiction such as the short stories "The Legend of Sleepy Hollow" and "Rip Van Winkle," he wrote several factual books that chronicled the exploits of the men who journeyed westward in the first half of the nineteenth century to trap beaver. Irving was deeply impressed with these historical figures, many of whom he met on his own travels west. In one book, Irving claimed:

A totally different class [of American hero] has now sprung up—"the Mountaineers," the traders and trappers that scale the

This nineteenth-century painting depicts a lone fur trapper riding on horseback in search of his quarry. Known as Mountain Men, such trappers were celebrated as heroes of the American wilderness.

vast mountain chains, and pursue their hazardous vocations amidst their wild recesses. [They are] hardy, lithe, vigorous, and active; extravagant in word, and thought, and deed; heedless of hardship [and] daring of danger. [Such] is the mountaineer, the hardy trapper of the West.[2]

Irving's lavish praise was for Smith and hundreds of other trappers who became known as Mountain Men or Mountaineers. The names stemmed from the Rocky Mountains, the tow-ering chain of mountain ranges through which these hardy adventurers relentlessly roamed in pursuit of the numerous beaver that inhabited its hundreds of streams and rivers.

The Mountain Men were heroes to Americans because they dared to live and trap beaver in a wilderness far removed from settled areas. In 1783, when the United States won its independence by defeating Great Britain in the American Revolution, the new nation consisted of thirteen former British colonies that lined the coast of the Atlantic Ocean. Several decades

The solitary nature of the Mountain Man's life is poignantly illustrated in this engraving depicting a trapper pausing at a stream to allow his horses to drink.

The Rocky Mountains, where the Mountain Men hunted for beaver, comprised a vast area of rugged wilderness in nineteenth-century America, as this painting illustrates.

later, there were still few Americans living west of the Mississippi River, and the huge area extending westward to the Rocky Mountains was considered an unknown wilderness.

Yet even in this period, U.S. leaders were dreaming of the day when their nation's borders would extend not just to the Rockies but all the way to the far-off Pacific Ocean. In 1819 Secretary of State John Quincy Adams, who five years later would be elected president, gave voice to this ambitious goal. In what amounted to a warning to other nations, the future president said: "The world shall [soon] be familiarized with the idea of considering our proper dominion to be the continent of North America. Europe shall [discover] that the United States and North America are identical."[3]

Before that could happen, however, Americans had to settle western areas that were only blank spots on maps because no one knew anything about them. It was the Mountain Men who would first venture into these unknown regions. And although they were seeking riches from beaver and other fur-bearing animals, they would play a vital role in fulfilling that prophecy of national growth. The reports that the Mountain Men brought back from their journeys through the West led many Americans to realize that these new lands would be good places to live because of their great beauty and abundant natural resources, such as timber and rich farmland. The Mountain Men also mapped these previously unknown regions. And the trails leading westward that trappers like Smith, Jim Bridger, and Joseph Reddeford Walker discovered enabled pioneers to move to the new areas and make them part of the United States.

A MOUNTAIN MAN'S VISION

Although most Mountain Men were more concerned with trapping beaver than building a nation, a few of them were aware of the future importance of the vast wilderness they roamed. In 1833, when Zenas Leonard accompanied Walker on a historic trip through California and Oregon, their group encountered Mexican and British officials who were already living there. In this period, both Mexico and Great Britain controlled areas that would one day become part of the United States. In *Adventures of Zenas Leonard: Fur Trader,* the memoir he wrote in 1839, Leonard warned the U.S. government about the threat these other nations posed to American ownership of the new lands. "Our government," he wrote, "should be vigilant. She should assert her claim by taking possession of the whole territory as soon as possible."[4] Leonard issued that advice to his nation's leaders because he also had a dream for the future that rivaled the one Adams had articulated two decades earlier. Claimed Leonard: "Most of this vast waste of territory belongs to the Republic of the United States. What a theme to contemplate its settlement and civilization. We have good reason to suppose that the territory west of the mountain will some day be equally as important to a nation as that on the east."[5]

Few Mountain Men possessed Leonard's historical vision. However, they all played an important part in helping the United States become the nation it is today.

CHAPTER 1

THE FUR TRADE IN U.S. HISTORY

Despite its importance to the westward expansion of the United States, the Mountain Man era was relatively short, lasting only a few decades in the first half of the nineteenth century. This key historic period ended in the early 1840s, when the low price of beaver pelts and the increasing scarcity of this valuable mammal put an end to wide-scale trapping. There is some disagreement, however, on when the era in which Mountain Men dominated the far west began. A few historians claim that it started in 1807, when Manuel Lisa became the first to lead fur trappers westward out of St. Louis, Missouri, toward the Rocky Mountains. Most historians, however, date the onset of this era to February 13, 1822, when the following advertisement appeared in the *Gazette and Public Advertiser* newspaper in St. Louis:

TO ENTERPRISING YOUNG MEN The subscriber wishes to

This engraving projects a romanticized image of a Mountain Man, with long, scraggly hair, unkempt beard, and a rifle slung over his shoulder.

engage ONE HUNDRED MEN, to ascend the river Missouri to its source, there to be employed for one, two, or three years. For particulars enquire of Major Andrew Henry (who will ascend with, and command, the party) or to the subscriber at St. Louis. Wm. H. Ashley.[6]

The ad was placed by William Ashley and Andrew Henry, who were seeking trappers for their fledgling Rocky Mountain Fur Company (RMFC). Within a month, they had hired workers and dispatched them to the far-off Rockies. Legendary Mountain Men like Jim Bridger, Jedediah Smith, Milton Sublette, Thomas Fitzpatrick, Henry Fraeb, James Clyman, and Hugh Glass helped the RMFC become the era's most important trapping concern.

When Ashley and Henry the following summer brought a huge load of beaver pelts back to St. Louis, the fur trade's eastern hub, their success sparked development of similar trapping ventures. In the next two decades, hundreds of trappers streamed into the Rocky Mountains annually to trap beaver and explore unknown areas that would one day become part of the United States.

WHY BECOME A MOUNTAIN MAN?

The Mountain Men who answered Ashley and Henry's advertisement in 1822 as well as others who went west to trap beaver all wanted to make money. However, many of them had additional reasons for risking their lives by venturing into the unknown, dangerous wilderness. The complex emotions that motivated them are exemplified by those that led eighteen-year-old Warren Angus Ferris to head west in 1829 from his native Buffalo, New York. After making his way to St. Louis, Ferris joined the American Fur Company and journeyed into the Rocky Mountains. In the book Ferris wrote about his five years as a Mountaineer, he explains that even he was not sure why he went:

> Westward! Ho! It is the sixteenth [day] of the second month A. D. 1830 and I have joined a trapping, trading, hunting expedition to the Rocky Mountains. Why, I scarcely know, for the motives that induced me to this step were of a mixed complexion. Curiosity, a love of wild adventure, and perhaps also a hope of profit, for times are hard . . . combined to make me look upon the project with an eye of favor.[7]

Economics did play a part in helping Ferris make his decision; he notes in his book that his coat was so shabby by the time he reached St. Louis that he was ashamed of his appearance. Ferris, however, was seeking more than money. Like most people who headed west, Ferris was burning with

❧ THE LURE OF FREEDOM ❧

In 1846, seventeen-year-old Lewis H. Garrard left St. Louis to see the western frontier. In his travels through the Southwest and the Rockies, Garrard met Kit Carson and other Mountain Men. In Wah-to-Yah and the Taos Trail, *which he wrote several years later, Garrard explained that Mountain Men wanted to live as freely as possible, to be self-sufficient, and to be left alone by other people. Garrard also detailed advice he got on how to be accepted by Mountain Men:*

To judge by his frankness and reckless life, his sole aim appears to be freedom of person & speech in its fullest import. [In the wilderness] one experiences a grand sensation of liberty and a total absence of fear; nobody to say what one shall do. No conventional rules of society restrict him to any particular form of dress, manner, or speech; he can swear a blue streak, or pray; it is his own affair entirely. The [newcomer to the frontier] is often reminded, amid showers of maledictions [curses], to confine his philanthropic deeds and conversations to his own dear self. I was quite amused by the kindly intentioned remarks of an old mountaineer to me, shortly after my appearance in the country: "If you see a man's mule running off, don't stop it—let it go; it isn't your'n. If his possible sack [bag of personal possessions] falls off, don't tell him of it; he'll find it out. At camp, help cook—get wood and water—make yourself active—get your pipe and smoke it—don't ask too many questions, and you'll pass!

---

desire to explore the vast, untamed wilderness.

That same fierce urge to explore unknown areas also motivated twenty-three-year-old Jedediah Smith to travel to St. Louis from Pennsylvania in 1823 and start working for Ashley and Henry. An explanation Smith wrote years later provides insight into why he became a Mountain Man: "I, of course expected to find Beaver, which with us hunters is a primary object, but I was also led on by the love of novelty common to all, which is much increased by the pursuit of its gratification."[8]

In addition to wanting to experience new things and see new lands, many people who became Mountain Men were also seeking personal freedom. In the western wilderness there was no one to tell them how they should dress, think, or act. For example, most trappers defied conventional ideas about clothing by adopting Native American styles. They wore moccasins, deerskin shirts, and in winter heavy buffalo robes because this type of clothing was practical for the way they lived and worked.

One Mountain Man, Bill Hamilton, insisted that risk and hardship were worth the chance to live an unrestricted life: "I have often been asked why we exposed ourselves to such danger. My answer has always been that there was a charm in the life of a free mountaineer from which one cannot free himself, after he once has fallen under its spell."[9]

Like many people who headed west in the nineteenth century, some Mountain Men, like Christopher "Kit" Carson, were also running away from a life they hated. Carson was born in 1809 and his father died eight years later, leaving his widow and eight children to lead a life of poverty on their small farm. Carson was apprenticed at age fourteen to a saddle-maker in Franklin, Missouri, but hated the job so much that he ran away after several years rather than "pass my life in labor that was distasteful to me."[10] Carson joined a wagon train traveling to Santa Fe, then a Mexican possession, and a few years later headed into the Rocky Mountains.

Carson became famous for trapping beaver and guiding military expeditions that mapped much of the Southwest, and during his lifetime many books and newspaper stories were written about him. Ironically, his name first appeared in print in the *Missouri Intelligencer* of October 12,

Christopher "Kit" Carson became famous for guiding expeditions that mapped out the American Southwest.

1826, when David Workman, his employer, listed Carson as a runaway in an advertisement seeking his return. It read: "Christopher Carson, a boy about sixteen years old, small of his age, but thick set, light hair, ran away from the subscriber to whom he had been bound to learn the saddler's trade. . . . One cent reward will be given to any person who will bring back the said boy."[11] No one hunted down the youth to claim the penny reward and stop him from heading west to carve a niche for himself in U.S. history. But before Carson and the other Mountain Men flocked to the Rocky Mountains in the early nineteenth century, other adventurous young men had been writing the history of the North American fur trade for several centuries.

EARLY FUR TRADE

When the first European settlers arrived in the New World in the late 1500s, trapping and selling furs immediately became an important way for them to make money. Animal skins and hides were valuable in Europe because centuries of hunting had brought fur-bearing animals there to the brink of extinction. Although the New World teemed with otter, mink, lynx, and other animals with exotically beautiful fur, beaver was the most sought after. The reason for the popularity of this humble, water-dwelling animal was that its rich, heavy fur could be processed into felt to make several types of apparel, especially dress hats for gentlemen, which came into fashion in the mid-1500s. So many beaver skins were used to make the popular hats, which were nicknamed a "beaver," that by 1600 few of the animals were left in Europe.

This scarcity in the seventeenth century made beaver pelts a major source

Beavers were extremely plentiful in the American West. Their coveted pelts brought a fortune to those hardy enough to become fur trappers.

of revenue for French and English colonists. They traded metal knives and kettles, cloth, and other inexpensive items to Native Americans for furs and sold them at a profit in Europe. Even the Pilgrims began trading and selling furs after they landed at Plymouth Rock in 1620. They sent so many pelts to England that by 1632 beaver were becoming scarce in Massachusetts; they were also rapidly disappearing in other English and French colonies.

SEARCHING FOR BEAVER

As beaver became scarce in settled areas, French and English traders had to travel further west to find them. It was in this way that much of North America was first explored. French traders who voyaged by canoe and on foot across much of modern-day Canada and the northern United States were the first Europeans to travel on the Great Lakes of Michigan and Superior as well as the Mississippi River.

One of the most important of these explorations came in 1793 when Alexander Mackenzie of Scotland travelled west across the continent to the Pacific Ocean. Mackenzie was employed by the North West Company, an English fur-trading firm. He reached Puget Sound in present-day Washington on July 22, 1793, after a long, difficult journey in which he and his party walked and canoed thousands of miles. In 1801 Mackenzie wrote *Voyages from Montreal Through the Continent of North America*, an account of the historic trip. In his book, Mackenzie theorized that the fur trade could help the British gain control of parts of North America that Americans had not yet settled: "By opening the [fur trade] between the Atlantic and Pacific and forming regular establishments through the interior and at both extremes [coasts of the continent] it would create the field for commercial enterprise and incalculable [good] would be the produce of it."[12] Mackenzie had hoped his book would spur the British to secure more territory in North America. Instead, it became a catalyst for U.S. exploration and eventual settlement of the West. This happened because President Thomas Jefferson read Mackenzie's book soon after it was published.

A DREAM OF U.S. EXPANSION

Jefferson himself had long nurtured a deep personal desire to push America's borders west to the Pacific Ocean. It was a bold dream because the country he headed was less than two decades old and consisted of only sixteen states, none of whose borders extended more than a few hundred miles west of the Atlantic Ocean.

The United States of America came into existence in 1783 when American colonists won their freedom by defeating Great Britain in the American Revolution. Under the Treaty of Paris

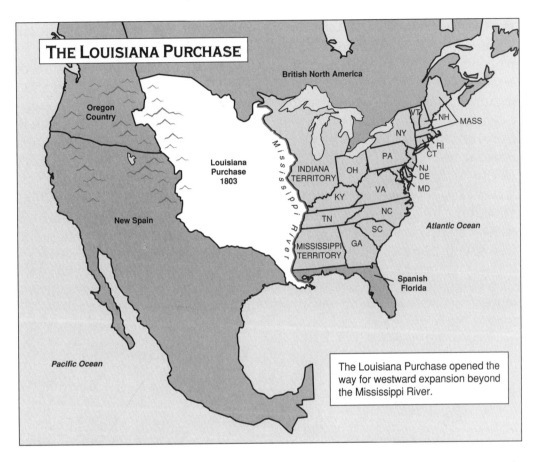

THE LOUISIANA PURCHASE

British North America

Oregon
Country

Louisiana
Purchase
1803

Mississippi River

New Spain

INDIANA
TERRITORY

OH

PA

VT
NH   MASS

NY

RI
CT

NJ
DE
MD

KY

VA

TN

NC

SC

MISSISSIPPI
TERRITORY

GA

Atlantic Ocean

Spanish
Florida

Pacific Ocean

The Louisiana Purchase opened the
way for westward expansion beyond
the Mississippi River.

that ended the war, the new nation was granted a huge chunk of unsettled British territory that extended west to the Mississippi River. At the time, however, the land beyond the river was claimed by France, Spain, and Great Britain. The French had recently acquired Louisiana, a vast wilderness territory between the Mississippi River and the Rocky Mountains. Spain ruled Mexico, California, and an area in the Southwest that included the future states of Texas, Arizona, and Nevada. Great Britain controlled Canada and was claiming the right to settle Oregon Country, a Pacific Coast area that today includes the states of Oregon and Washington.

In 1803 Jefferson took an important step to extend the nation's borders when he ordered U.S. officials to begin negotiations to buy Louisiana from France, which a year earlier had received the area from Spain. On May 2, 1803, the United States doubled its size by purchasing Louisiana's 800 million acres of land for $15 million or about 1.8 cents an acre.

A HISTORIC EXPEDITION

To further his dream of westward expansion, the nation's third president sent an expedition to explore the new territory. Jefferson chose Meriwether Lewis and William Clark to lead the Corps of Discovery, a team that would travel from St. Louis to the Pacific Ocean. Because Jefferson knew that Americans could not move west to settle those areas until they had a reliable way to travel there, he ordered Lewis and Clark to scout out "the most direct & practicable water [route] across the continent."[13]

Lewis and Clark left St. Louis on May 14, 1804. The Corps of Discovery concluded its historic cross-country journey in November 1805 when its members canoed down the Columbia River to the Pacific Ocean in present-day Oregon. To their surprise, Lewis and Clark found that some Indians there spoke a few English words, which they had learned from sailors on ships that had been arriving for

This drawing depicts Sacagawea leading Lewis and Clark and the Corps of Discovery on their journey west. Their expedition took them from St. Louis to the Oregon coast.

several years. In his January 9, 1806, journal entry, Lewis commented: "The persons who usually visit the entrance of this river for the purpose of [trading for furs] I believe are either English or Americans; the Indians inform us that they speak the same language with ourselves."[14]

English and American ships had been visiting the Pacific Coast since the late 1700s to obtain furs, which they carried to China and exchanged for silk, tea, and other products. One of the early visitors was Robert Gray, a ship captain from Boston, Massachusetts. On May 11, 1792, Gray became the first to sail up the mouth of the Columbia River, which he named after his ship, the *Columbia*. Gray's arrival gave the United States its first legitimate claim to U.S. possession of the area, and Lewis and Clark's overland journey more than a decade later strengthened it. This would be important in the next few decades as the United States and Great Britain vied for control of the so-called Oregon Country.

Although Lewis and Clark were amazed to find Indians who spoke English, they understood that the ships had stopped to trade because the region had many fur-bearing animals. They had found the same abundance of such animals throughout the great wilderness they were exploring. After their triumphant return, Lewis sent a letter to President Jefferson in which he reported on the rich harvest of fur awaiting American trappers: "The portion of the continent watered by the Missouri [River] and its branches from the Cheyenne [River] upward is richer in beaver and otter than any country on earth, particularly that portion of its subsidiary streams lying within the Rocky Mountains."[15]

RUSH FOR FURS

The reports about fur-bearing animals that Lewis and Clark issued when they finally made it back to St. Louis on September 23, 1806, two years and four months after they had left, ignited new interest in the West. During the following winter, fur traders gathered in St. Louis and made preparations to travel up the Missouri River to trap beaver.

The most important trader was Manuel Lisa, who in the spring of 1807 left St. Louis with a supply of cloth, knives, and other items he would give Indians for their furs. Lisa hired John Colter and Louis Drouillard, who had been members of the Lewis and Clark expedition, to guide Lisa's party to the confluence of the Yellowstone and Bighorn rivers in what is today central Montana. Lisa built a trading post there that he named Fort Manuel and traded successfully with Crow Indians. He returned to St. Louis in the summer of 1808 with enough beaver pelts to induce several wealthy men to join him in starting the

❧ MANUEL LISA: ❧
THE FIRST MOUNTAIN MAN

Manuel Lisa was the first of the great Mountain Men who roamed the Rocky Mountains seeking wealth in the form of beaver pelts. Lisa was born of Spanish parents on September 8, 1772, in New Orleans, then a possession of Spain, and by 1800 he was trading with Indians for furs. In 1807, Lisa led the first large group of trappers up the Missouri River and began trading for beaver pelts with Crow Indians and other tribes. Lisa was so successful that other fur traders claimed he cheated Indians out of furs. In 1817, Lisa discussed the charge in a letter to the explorer William Clark, who was now governor of the Louisiana Territory. In this excerpt from his letter, from the second volume of The American Fur Trade of the Far West *by Hiram Martin Chittenden, Lisa justifies his success:*

I have had some success as a trader; and this gives rise to many reports [such as] "Manuel gets so much rich fur!" Well, I will explain how I get it. First, I put into my operations great activity; I go a great distance while some [of his competitors] are considering whether they will start today or tomorrow. I impose upon myself great privations; ten months in a year I am buried in the forest, at a vast distance from my own house. I appear as the benefactor, and not as the pillager, of the Indians. . . . My establishments [trading forts] are the refuge of the weak and of the old men no longer able to . . . [care for themselves], and by these means I have acquired the confidence and friendship of these nations, and the consequent choice of their trade.

Missouri Fur Company. Lisa ventured into the Rockies at least a dozen times before his death in 1820, traveling an estimated 26,000 miles, and making a small fortune in the Rocky Mountain fur trade.

Lisa's efforts, however, were soon dwarfed by those of New York businessman John Jacob Astor, one of the world's richest men. His desire to dominate the fur trade led him to establish the first U.S. enterprise on the West Coast.

ASTORIA

Astor was born in Germany but emigrated to the United States in 1783 at the age of twenty. Settling in New York, he began buying pelts and skins and selling them in Europe. The reports by Lewis and Clark convinced Astor that he could make money buying furs from Native Americans in the West. In 1808 he founded the American Fur Company, which was based in New York and gathered furs in frontier areas west to the Rocky

Mountains. Because Astor wanted to dominate the entire continent's fur trade, he also decided to establish a branch of his business on the west coast at the mouth of the Columbia River. Even though he was wealthy and influential, Astor wrote to President Jefferson to get the president's approval for his new business. Jefferson replied that he believed Astor's fur business could help the nation's westward expansion by establishing a western trading outpost manned by Americans: "I [favor] the commencement of a settlement on that point of the western coast of America, and look forward with gratification to the time when its descendants should have spread themselves through the whole length of that coast, covering it with free and independent Americans."[16]

Astor began his bid to control the nation's fur trade in 1811 by dispatching two expeditions, one by land and one by sea. The *Tonquin* sailed from New York to the mouth of the Columbia River, where workers began building Astoria, a trading fort named for Astor. It was located on Point George on the southern shore of the river near the location of Fort Clatsop, the camp that Lewis and Clark had built and lived in during the winter of 1805–06. At the same time the *Tonquin* was sailing to Oregon, Wilson Price Hunt began leading a large party overland to the Columbia. Hunt's mission was to scout out sites for a series of trading forts that Astor wanted to build across the continent.

Both ventures were marred by tragedy. After reaching the Columbia, the *Tonquin* sailed north to trade with Indians and landed at Nootka Sound

Intent on dominating North America's fur trade, John Jacob Astor founded the American Fur Company in 1802.

on Vancouver Island. When Captain Jonathan Thorne struck an Indian chief during an argument, tribal members retaliated by killing the ship's crew. The overland Astorians became lost several times, ran out of supplies, and struggled with bad weather on their brutal trip west; several men died of exposure, one went mad, and the survivors did not reach the Columbia until January 1812. Despite such severe problems, Astor succeeded in establishing an American presence on the West Coast and his men began ac-

quiring furs. Alexander Ross, one of Astor's most trusted employees, explains how he began trading with Indians in 1811:

I sent messages to the different tribes around, who soon assembled, bringing with them their furs. The number of Indians collected on the occasion could not have been less than 2,000. [So] anxious were they to trade, and so fond of tobacco, that one morning before breakfast I ob-

---

ॐ ASTORIA ॐ

Astoria, the trading fort that workers for John Jacob Astor's American Fur Company built in 1811 in present-day Oregon, was important because it was the first permanent U.S. settlement on the western coast. Alexander Ross was a clerk who helped supervise construction of the fort, whose tall walls protected the residents against attacks by Native Americans. In this excerpt from Westward Expansion: An Eyewitness History *by Sanford Wexler, Ross explains how difficult it was to build the fort:*

The [sea] with its rocky shores, lay in front; the breakers on the [sand]bar, rolling in wild confusion, closed the view on the west; on the east, the country [had] a wild and varied aspect, while towards the south, the im-

pervious and magnificent forest darkened the landscape as far as the eye could reach. The place selected for the emporium of the West might challenge the whole continent to produce a spot [that presented] more difficulties to the settler: studded with gigantic trees of almost incredible size, many of them measuring fifty feet in girth, and so close together, and intermingled with huge rocks, as to make it a work of no ordinary labor to level and clear the ground. With this task before us every man, from the highest to the lowest, was armed with an axe in one hand and a gun in the other: the former for attacking the woods, the latter for defense against [Indians] which were constantly prowling about.

tained 110 beavers for leaf tobacco, at the rate of five leaves per skin; and at last, when I had but one yard of white cotton [cloth] remaining, one of the chiefs gave me twenty prime beaver skins for it.[17]

The War of 1812, however, doomed Astor's venture. After Great Britain and the United States began fighting in June, members of the British North West Company visited Astoria and demanded that Astor's men sell them the fort and all its holdings. Even though Astor's men did not want to sell to their British fur rival, they had little choice because the *Phoebe*, an English warship, was anchored nearby and could have destroyed Astoria.

THE FUR TRADE'S REBIRTH

The war marked the beginning of several years of stagnation in the North American fur trade. Until the fighting ended in 1815, Americans had trouble selling furs in Europe because English warships stopped U.S. vessels from sailing there. The war was followed by a worldwide economic downturn that depressed fur prices and made the trade unprofitable.

As economic conditions improved in the early 1820s, interest in the fur trade revived. The most important firm to emerge in this period was the Rocky Mountain Fur Company, founded by veteran frontiersmen Ashley and Henry. When the trappers they sent into the Rockies began sending large packets of beaver skins back to St. Louis, the future of the Rocky Mountain fur trade was assured. Hundreds of trappers began journeying into the Rockies and within a few years they were harvesting up to 100,000 beaver skins each year.

The RMFC and other firms had no trouble finding workers in St. Louis, a rough frontier town that attracted many men who wanted to head into the wilderness that lay beyond it. The hiring of James Clyman is typical of the informal way companies recruited trappers. After working as a surveyor in Illinois, Clyman was in St. Louis in February 1824 when he heard that Ashley needed men. When Clyman went to Ashley's home to inquire about a job, Ashley explained that it involved trapping beaver. Clyman later wrote of his visit with Ashley: "[He] gave a lengthy account of game found in that Region [including] immense Quantities of Beaver whose skins were very valuable selling from $5 to $8 per pound at that time in St. Louis and the men he wished to engage were to [be] hunters [and] trappers."[18] Clyman did not take a job right away because he had just been paid for his surveying job and wanted to enjoy himself drinking and gambling in St. Louis. After spending all his money, Clyman worked for Ashley for several years as a trapper.

ROCKY MOUNTAIN INVASION

The fur industry grew quickly in the pivotal year of 1822 after Ashley and Henry committed their new firm to venturing into the Rocky Mountains. This fact was proudly noted in the September 17, 1822, edition of the *Missouri Intelligencer* newspaper: "Those formerly engaged in the trade have increased their capital and extended their enterprise, many new firms have engaged in it and others are preparing to do so. [It] is computed that a thousand men chiefly from this place [St. Louis] are now employed [in the fur trade]."[19]

CHAPTER 2

HOW MOUNTAIN MEN TRAPPED BEAVER

Of all the groups of trappers and traders seeking their fortune in furs, none was more important than the Rocky Mountain Fur Company (RMFC). In addition to initiating the Mountain Man era's peak years of trapping and exploration, the firm that William Ashley and Andrew Henry founded in 1822 changed the way in which the fur business itself was conducted. Instead of trading with Indians as other firms had done for centuries, the RMFC sent trappers into the Rocky Mountains to harvest the beaver pelts themselves. Ashley and Henry decided to do this because of the expense of building and maintaining trading forts so far from St. Louis and because some Indians in the Rockies opposed the presence of the whites and did not want to trade with them.

Although trapping instead of trading was a revolutionary development in the fur trade, rival firms quickly adopted the RMFC's new method in the beaver-rich Rockies. This was true even for John Jacob Astor's American Fur Company, which had been forced to leave the west coast during the War of 1812 and had then dominated the fur trade east of the Rockies by setting up a chain of forts on the upper Missouri River. On October 24, 1831, a St. Louis resident named Thomas Forsyth explained this historic change to Lewis Cass, President Andrew Jackson's secretary of war, who had inquired about the current state of the fur industry. Forsyth told Cass that Ashley and Henry had transformed the fur trade: "From what I can learn, there is but little trading [with Indians] done on either side of the Rocky Mountains. It is altogether by hunting that they collect so many furs."[20]

Forsyth also explained to Cass that since 1882, when Ashley and Henry had begun sending men into the

Fur trappers set up steel traps to catch beaver in this nineteenth-century painting. Such devices trapped beaver by clamping down on the animal's foot like a pair of metal jaws.

Rockies to trap beaver, they and other U.S. fur companies that copied their method had begun to dominate British rivals like the Hudson's Bay Company. Wrote Forsyth:

> Perhaps it would not be exceeding the truth to say that half a million of dollars in furs [a sum that today would be worth many times that] are now brought down the Missouri River that formerly went to Hudson's Bay, and it is the enterprising spirit of Ashley which has occasioned the change of this channel of trade.[21]

The result of this innovation in gathering furs was that more beaver pelts were collected than ever before, more than 100,000 annually in the peak years of the Mountain Man period. In order to take so many pelts, however, trappers had to stay year-round in the wilderness areas where they worked. This new way of doing business thus created a new way of life for these men, who soon became known as Mountaineers or Mountain Men.

ROCKY MOUNTAIN TRAPPING

The Rocky Mountains are a continuous chain of scores of mountain ranges that extend southward some four thousand miles from the Canadian border to New Mexico. A few of the ranges that make up the Rockies are the Big

Horn and Coeur d'Alene in Montana, Bitterroot in Idaho, Teton in Wyoming, Sangre de Cristo in New Mexico, and Sawatch in Colorado. These towering mountain ranges have individual peaks more than twenty thousand feet tall but are dotted with beaver-rich valleys and plateaus. It was in these areas that Mountain Men lived and worked, often for several years at a time.

Although some men trapping beaver were hired by fur companies, most Mountain Men were "free trappers," independent workers who sold their furs to anyone. Among the latter group were some of the period's most legendary figures, such as Jim Bridger, Kit Carson, and Jedediah Smith. It was the independent trappers who most impressed Captain Benjamin Louis Bonneville during the leave of absence he took from the U.S. Army in 1832 to explore the West and trap beaver. Bonneville said with admiration of free trappers: "They come and go when and where they please; provide their own horses, arms, and other equipment; trap and trade on their own account; and dispose of their skins and peltries to the highest bidder."[22]

In their pursuit of beaver pelts, trappers roamed wherever they wanted throughout the vast expanse of the Rocky Mountains. However, they usually traveled in large groups because of the constant threat of attacks by Native Americans who were angry that strangers were invading land they considered their own. Fur companies sent their hired trappers into the mountains in groups of forty to sixty men called "brigades." Free trappers banded together in similar-sized parties and sometimes paid a small fee for the right to travel with company-sponsored brigades.

As the Mountain Men roamed the Rockies to trap beaver, they fell into a year-long routine that included spring and fall hunting seasons and a dormant period during the coldest months of winter. The highlight of each year was the rendezvous, a wild and raucous summer get-together at a spot in the mountains agreed on by all the fur companies. The event was named with the French term for an appointment or date. It was held in the warmest part of summer, the period when beaver pelts were nearly worthless because the animals had shed much of their fur because of the heat.

At the rendezvous, Mountain Men traded their pelts to fur companies for money and supplies for the coming year of trapping, everything from coffee and sugar to gunpowder and lead to make bullets. The fur companies hauled tons of goods into the wilderness by wagon, boat, and horse so the trappers could stay in the Rockies and continue to trap beaver.

FINDING BEAVER

The end of each rendezvous marked the start of another year of trapping.

As they headed back into the mountains, the Mountain Men went to areas where they knew from past experience there were many beaver. Trappers never told anyone else where they were going and on their journeys often tried to conceal their tracks so other trappers could not follow them. They did this because the fur of beavers was so valuable that their pelts were known

---

❧ WINTER BEAVER HUNTING ❧

Mountain Men normally did not trap beaver after the rivers and streams of the Rocky Mountains froze over in winter because the work was so much harder than during the rest of the year. On rare occasions, however, they did trap beaver in the dead of winter. The River of the West, *which was based on author Frances A. Fuller Victor's interviews with Mountain Man Joe Meek, includes an explanation of how this was done. This excerpt is from an electronic version of her book on the* Mountain Man and the Fur Trade Virtual Research Center *Web site:*

The trapping season is usually in the spring and autumn. But should the hunters find it necessary to continue their work in winter, they capture the beaver by sounding [rapping] on the ice until an aperture is discovered, when the ice is cut away and the opening closed up. Returning to the bank, they search for the subterranean passage [leading to the room the beaver lives in], tracing its connection with the lodge; and by patient watching succeed in catching the beaver on some of its journeys between the water and the land. This, however, is not often resorted to when the hunt in the fall has been successful; or when not urged by famine to take the beaver for food.

Wearing snowshoes, a trapper in search of beaver makes his way through the forest in the dead of winter.

as "hairy bank notes." Osborne Russell, a trapper for nearly a decade, explained the cautious way his group left one rendezvous: "All had turned to the right or left without once hinting their intentions [of where they were going] for it was not good policy for a Trapper to let too many know where he intends to set his traps, particularly if his horse is not so fast as those of his companions."[23]

But when the Mountaineers arrived at their chosen spots, they sometimes discovered that other trappers had already decimated the beaver population. This happened in 1824 to James Ohio Pattie. Even though it was only two years after trappers had begun surging into the Rockies, Pattie's party discovered few beaver remaining at the spot they had chosen. Said Pattie: "We reached the Yellow Stone [River], and ascended it to its head; and thence crossed the ridges of the Rocky Mountains to Clarke's fork of the Columbia [River]. But all these streams had been so much trapped, as to yield but few beavers."[24]

Despite their disappointment, it was not hard for Pattie and his fellow trappers to travel on and find more sites populated by beaver. All they had to do was follow a river or stream to a spot where the aquatic animals had felled trees into the water to make a dam. In the tangle of trees that formed the dam, the beavers constructed lodges, structures made from small branches and dried mud that housed them and protected them from wolves and other natural enemies. The dams and lodges were so big that they were easy to find. But trappers could also recognize the beaver's footprints and interpret other signs of their habitation in order to quickly estimate how many beaver were in the area.

When the hunting party had located a spot rich with beaver, they made a base camp. Trappers would ride out from the camp each day to set traps near the streams where the beaver lived and collect the animals they had caught. As trappers began reducing the beaver population near their base camp, several of them might leave it for several days to hunt beaver further away. When an area had yielded up most of its beaver, the group would move to a new site.

TRAPPING BEAVER

Of the two hunts each year, the spring hunt was usually the more profitable because beaver pelts were thick with winter fur. To catch beaver, trappers used steel traps that weighed about five pounds and were attached to a chain some five feet long. The traps functioned like a metal jaw that would clamp down on the foot of the beaver to capture it. Trappers placed their traps in a section of a stream where beavers regularly went in and out of the water. Joe Meek, one of the most famous Rocky Mountain Fur Company

A pair of trappers return to a trap they had set, finding a beaver. The trappers used the beavers' own musk to lure them to the traps.

trappers, described how Mountain Men set traps:

> The trapper wades out into the stream, which is shallow, and cuts with his knife a bed for the trap, five or six inches under water. He then takes the trap pole [a heavy stick] out the whole length of the chain in the direction of the center of the stream, and drives it into the mud, so fast that the beaver cannot draw it out; at the same time tying the other end by a thong to the bank. A small stick or twig, dipped in musk or castor[e]um, serves for bait, and is placed so as to hang directly above the trap, which is now set.[25]

Castoreum is a pungent substance that beavers secrete from their glands to mark an area as their own; trappers got this smelly liquid from beavers they had already trapped. When a beaver smelled the castoreum, it would be curious enough to come close and investigate the stick. In doing so, the beaver usually stepped in the center of the trap, triggering the spring that snapped the metal jaws shut on its foot. The natural inclination of a beaver in danger is to swim to deeper water. But when a beaver caught in a

❧ THE BEAVER ❧

During the Mountain Man era, many people considered beaver the wisest of all animals because they were smart enough to fell trees to build homes. In Washington Irving's Adventures of Captain Bonneville, *Benjamin Louis Bonneville, who led a party that trapped beaver and explored the Rocky Mountains, discounts claims that beaver were smart enough to make trees fall where they wanted them:*

Captain Bonneville discredits, on the whole, the alleged sagacity of the beaver in this particular, and thinks the animal has no other aim than to get the tree down, without any of the subtle calculation as to its mode or direction of falling. This attribute, he thinks, has been ascribed to them from the circumstance that [the beaver simply] attacks those trees which are nearest at hand, and on the banks of the stream or pond. He makes incisions round them, or in technical phrase, belts them with his teeth, and when they fall, they naturally take the direction in which their trunks or branches preponderate. "I have often," says Captain Bonneville, "seen trees at the places where they had been cut through by the beaver, but they lay in all directions, and often very inconveniently for the after purposes of the animal. In fact, so little ingenuity do they at times display in this particular, that at one of our camps on Snake River, a beaver was found with his head wedged into the cut which he had made, the tree having fallen upon him and held him prisoner until he died."

Beavers build their homes from trees they fell themselves.

trap did that, the heavy metal weighed the animal down and it would drown.

The trappers came back each day to collect the dead beavers and set the traps again. If the beaver in its death struggles had managed to free the trap from the pole that anchored it in the stream, trappers could usually find the trap if it was still nearby. This was possible because each trap had a float stick attached to it, a piece of wood on a hide thong that floated on the surface of the water and could be seen even if the trap had sunk in deep water.

Trappers were usually able to take several beaver from the same area. However, as animals disappeared from the beaver colony, the survivors began to sense that something dangerous was happening and would stay away from traps placed in the water. When this happened, trappers usually tried a different way to catch them. They began placing traps in the paths beavers used on land, concealing them so the animals would accidentally step on them. However, the beavers often were able to figure out what was happening, avoid the traps, and sometimes even render them useless. When this happened, Mountain Men said that the beavers were "up to trap" and quit trying to trap them in that area. Bonneville explained how beavers could disable traps:

The beaver now approaches [the traps] cautiously, and springs

them ingeniously with a stick. At other times, he turns the traps bottom upwards, by the same means, and occasionally even drags them [away] and conceals them in the mud. The trapper now gives up the contest of ingenuity, and shouldering his traps, marches off, admitting that he [has been beaten].[26]

Trappers usually had only enough time to maintain six traps on a daily basis. They had to travel between the traps, which could be located several miles apart, set them again, and skin the beavers they had caught. Trappers cut the pelts off beavers right away because they were too heavy to carry back to camp. While an adult beaver weighed between thirty and sixty pounds, a pelt was only one-and-a-half to two pounds. Although the trappers usually left the animal carcasses behind, they sometimes took beaver tails back to their camps because they considered beaver tail meat a delicacy.

TRAPPING FROM CANOES

Mountain Men usually trapped beaver while working from a land base camp. However, they sometimes hunted while paddling canoes and other types of vessels down the rivers and streams that were their quarry's natural habitat. When trappers used these waterways to explore new territory or make a long journey, they often set traps at

A team of trappers paddles their canoe along the Missouri River in search of beaver. Once they come upon an area populated by beavers, they will set their traps.

night so they could continue to make some money while they traveled.

An example of this kind of waterborne trapping occurred in 1829 when James Pattie and a group of other trappers traveled down the Red River (in modern-day New Mexico) and stopped to trap whenever they came upon beaver habitats:

> We floated about 30 miles, and in the evening encamped in the midst of signs of beavers. We set 40 traps, and in the morning of [December] 10th caught 36 beavers, an excellent night's hunt. We concluded from this encouraging commencement, to travel slowly, and in hunters' phrase, trap the river clear; that is, take all that could be allured to come to the bait.[27]

Pattie did not identify what kind of craft his group used. However, because his book states that the trappers made it themselves, it was probably a dugout, a primitive canoe made by hollowing out a log. To travel by water, trappers also relied heavily on bull boats, which were made from dried buffalo hides stretched tight over willow branches. Although both of these simple vessels were sometimes hard to maneuver and often tipped over, they were easy to build and easy to repair.

PREPARING THE PELT

Whether the trappers were riding horses or paddling a canoe, they had a lot of work to do after they trapped a beaver. After removing the beaver's fur, they had to cure (preserve) the pelt so it would not rot before it could be taken back east and sold. The first step in curing the pelt was the hardest. The trappers used the sharp edges of knives and axes to scrape all flesh and blood off the inner side of the fur. Although free trappers often had to do this task themselves, company brigades included men whose only job was to do rough chores such as cutting firewood and curing pelts. After the pelts were cleaned, they were stretched on frames made from tree branches and dried in the open air and sun. When Mountain Men were successful in their trapping, drying pelts would be hanging everywhere in the camp. In a book he wrote about his years as a trapper, Warren Angus Ferris recalled such a scene from a visit to a group of trappers led by Jim Bridger:

Their encampment was decked with hundreds of beaver skins, now drying in the sun. These valuable skins are always stretched in willow hoops, varying from eighteen inches, to three feet in diameter, according to the size of the skins, and have a reddish appearance on the flesh side, which

❧ BUILDING A BULL BOAT ❧

Mountain Men routinely traveled on streams and rivers in boats they built themselves. One of the most common was the bull boat, which was made of buffalo hides. John B. Wyeth, who in 1832 traveled from Boston to the Pacific coast, provides this description in Oregon: A Short History of a Long Journey from the Atlantic Ocean to the Region of the Pacific by Land:

They first cut a number of willows of about an inch and a half diameter at the butt end, and fixed them in the ground at proper distances from each other, and as they approached nearer one end they brought them nearer together, so as to form something like the bow. The ends of the whole were brought and bound firmly together, like the ribs of a great basket; and then they took other twigs of willow and wove them into those stuck in the ground so as to make a sort of firm, huge basket of twelve or fourteen feet long. After this was completed, they sewed together a number of buffalo-skins, and with them covered the whole; and after the different parts had been trimmed off smooth, a slow fire was made under the Bull-boat, taking care to dry the skins moderately; and as they gradually dried, and acquired a due degree of warmth, they rubbed buffalo tallow all over the outside of it, so as to allow it to enter into all the seams of the boat. As the melted tallow ran down into every seam, hole, and crevice, it cooled into a firm body capable of resisting the water, and bearing a considerable blow without damaging it.

is exposed to the sun. Our camps are always dotted with these red circles, in the trapping season, when the weather is fair.[28]

When the pelt was cleaned and dried, trappers marked it so they could identify it if it were stolen. This practice of marking pelts paid off in 1837 when a band of Crow Indians, who were normally friendly to whites, stole beaver skins from a group of trappers. When one of the trappers, Lucien Fontenelle, found out that the Crow had sold the furs to a trader named Antonio Montaro, he confronted the man at his trading post on the Powder River. In a letter to Osborne Russell, another of the trappers, Fontenelle explained how he got the furs back: "I ordered [Montaro] to give me the key to his warehouse, which he reluctantly did. I then ordered my clerk to go in and take all the beaver skins he could find with your names marked upon them, and to have them carried to my camp, which was done without further ceremony."[29]

The final step in preparing the beaver furs after they were cured and marked was to fold them in half, with the fur to the inside, and compact them into packs of about sixty pelts each. Trappers often built wooden presses to compress the furs, making the packs tighter and smaller. The finished packs weighed between ninety and one hundred pounds and were easy to trans-

port, either by water in boats or overland by horse and mule.

THE RENDEZVOUS

The fall hunt ended with the coming of the winter cold, which froze streams and rivers and made trapping nearly impossible. Mountain Men then headed to small, heavily wooded valleys that could shelter them during the harshest months of winter. When the snow and ice melted in spring, they moved out and began the spring trapping season. By July, the Mountain Men were not only ready for a vacation from the past year's difficult work but were running low on gunpowder and had long used up the last of their coffee and sugar. The remedy for both these problems was the annual rendezvous, which allowed them to stay in the wilderness for several years at a time.

The first rendezvous was in 1825 at Henry's Fork on the Green River in what is today Wyoming and the last was held in 1840, also on the Green River near present-day Horse Creek, Wyoming. Ashley and Henry began this annual event so they could resupply their trappers and collect their furs. Other companies soon began attending the annual get-together to get pelts from their own men and to compete to buy the furs of free trappers.

The various firms brought to the rendezvous what amounted to traveling department stores. Mountain Men traded their furs for a host of goods

This painting depicts a large rendezvous near the Green River in Wyoming. Both Mountain Men and Plains Indians can be seen trading pelts in the foreground.

they desperately needed, such as coffee, sugar, new traps, blankets, flannel shirts, and gunpowder. For trappers who might not have savored a cup of coffee in several months or who hungered for the taste of something sweet, the opportunity to satisfy such cravings made the rendezvous a joyous occasion. Because such items were in short supply even at this annual get-together, the fur companies tried to make sure everyone got a chance to stock up on supplies. Trapper Jim Beckwourth said that at the first rendezvous, Ashley refused to start swapping his supplies for furs until everyone who was expected

had shown up. According to Beckwourth, Ashley "would open none of his goods, except tobacco, until all had arrived, as he wished to make an equal distribution; for goods were then very scarce in the mountains and hard to obtain."[30]

Fur companies paid trappers by the pound for pelts. During the peak years of the Mountain Man era, this varied from $3 to $6. Although free trappers could earn $1,000 or more each year, a lot of money at the time, they spent most of what they got for their furs on supplies. At the 1830 rendezvous, for example, lead cost $1 a pound, gunpowder and coffee $1.50 a pound, and traps $9 each, an amount several times higher than the same purchase would have cost in St. Louis. The higher prices reflected the expense of hauling the goods over one thousand miles into the mountains as well as the risk involved in this long journey. Some loads of merchandise were lost in accidents, such as when boats sank, or stolen by Indians who attacked supply caravans.

BEAVER LINGO

The rendezvous marked both the end point of one trapping season and the beginning of a new one. But for the Mountain Men, daily life was one continuous, never-ending quest to locate and trap beaver. This animal's valuable fur coat had originally brought the Mountain Men west, and they spent each and every day afterward trapping beaver, preparing pelts they had taken, or making preparations for their next hunt. Thus it is no wonder that many of the terms trappers coined to communicate with each other contained the name of the animal that dominated their daily lives.

For example, trappers usually bought supplies and other merchandise with beaver fur instead of currency such as dollar bills. The prices they paid for furs and other items were established on the basis of "made beaver," meaning the dollar value of one cured beaver pelt. Thus a pound of coffee might sell for two "made beaver." The obsession with the small furry animal led to other terms involving its name: "gone beaver" was a person who had died; "to make beaver" meant to hurry up in traveling or other activities; "up to beaver" meant that a person was very smart. The last expression was a sign of the respect trappers had for the animal they hunted daily.

CHAPTER 3

THE HARD LIFE OF A MOUNTAIN MAN

Jedediah Smith's middle name was Strong. It was a fitting designation because it described one of the most important traits he and other Mountain Men needed to survive the many hardships they endured daily. Because they lived and worked year-round in the wilderness, Mountaineers had to provide their own shelter, food, and clothing. Although the hardy trappers often slept in the open protected only by blankets or buffalo robes, in winter they built cabins and Indian-style tepees for protection against the cold. They hunted buffalo and other animals for meat, which was the basis of their diet. The same quarry provided hides and fur from which they made hats, shirts, and footwear.

All those tasks required hard work. In the wilderness, even something as simple as lighting a fire to cook or stay warm could be difficult. Although people back east could easily start a fire by striking a match, Mountain Men rarely used matches because they were not only scarce but useless if they became wet. Instead, the Mountaineers banged a piece of steel against a chunk of flint to create a spark that ignited tinder, easily flammable material such as a handful of dry grass. They used the flame from the tinder to set twigs on fire and kept adding larger chunks of wood to produce a bigger blaze.

Making a fire was difficult if it was windy, wet, or very cold. In the winter of 1824, trappers James Clyman and Wilham Sublette were in danger of freezing to death when they woke up one bitterly cold morning and could not start a fire to warm themselves. Said Clyman: "As soon our hands became exposed to the air they became so numb that we could not hold the flint and steel [to create a spark]. We then [tried] our guns with no better success for the wind was so strong and for the want of some fine material [tinder] to catch the fire."[31] In desperation, Clyman dug his hand into the ashes of the large fire that had kept them warm the night before but had gone out while they slept. "To my Joy," Clyman said, "I found a small [bit] of fire alive not larger than a grain of corn. Throwing it in to [some dry material] I had gathered it started a blaze in a minuit and in one minuit more I had a fine fire."[32]

A Trapper's Outfit

Mountain Men were often on the move, searching for beaver, locating a place to spend the cold winter months, or making their way to the annual rendezvous. They could carry with them only what was essential to their survival. Osborne Russell, who spent a decade in the Rocky Mountains, describes the trapper's typical gear:

A Trappers equipments in such cases is generally one Animal upon which is placed . . . a riding Saddle and bridle a sack containing six Beaver traps a blanket with an extra pair of Mocasins his powder horn and bullet pouch with a belt to which is attached a butcher Knife a small wooden box containing bait for Beaver a

Dressed in buckskin clothing and fur hats, a team of trappers leads a horse laden with their provisions through a valley in the Rocky Mountains.

Tobacco sack with a pipe and implements for making fire with sometimes a hatchet fastened to the Pommel of his saddle.[33]

The Mountain Man's most important possession was his rifle. Trappers needed firearms to kill animals for food and to defend themselves against wild animals, hostile Indians, and sometimes other trappers. A Mountaineer's rifle generally had a thirty-four-inch barrel, which was shorter than that used in the East, but it had a larger diameter bore so it could fire a bigger, heavier lead ball weighing a

Armed with his rifle, his most treasured possession, a veteran Mountain Man rides alongside a horse carrying the rest of his gear.

half-ounce or more. These rifles had to be powerful enough to kill grizzly bears and other animals that were stronger and more dangerous than any back east. The Hawken, a model that was hand-crafted by brothers Jacob and Samuel Hawken in St. Louis, was the Mountain Man's favorite rifle.

The rifles and pistols Mountaineers carried were flintlock muzzle-loaders. The Mountain Men loaded the gun by pouring gunpowder down its muzzle (the open end of the barrel) and then ramming a round lead ball down on the powder. When he pulled the trigger, a curved metal hammer struck a piece of flint, creating a spark. This tiny burst of flame sent another spark through a small hole into the barrel, where it would ignite the main gunpowder charge. The resulting explosion generated gases that propelled the bullet from the barrel toward its target. Trappers made their own bullets by pouring molten lead into round molds.

The guns were heavy, weighing about twelve pounds, and accurate up to two hundred yards. In writing about Mountain Men, Washington Irving declared, "With his horse and his rifle, he is independent of the World, and spurns all its restraints."[34] Losing or damaging a rifle was a calamity to a Mountaineer because it left him defenseless and unable to hunt for food. This happened once to Warren Ferris: "I was thrown from my horse, by which my gun was broken so as to render it entirely useless. The feelings of a trapper may better be imagined than described, after losing his only means of subsistence and defense, in hourly danger of his life."[35]

The small amount of equipment every Mountain Man carried included a "possibles sack," a small leather bag that was usually secured around the neck by a strip of rawhide. It contained some of the trapper's most precious personal possessions, such as a pipe (which he kept even when he ran out of tobacco), a letter or picture from a loved one, and a spare flint and steel to make fire.

Although trappers only had tools and weapons they could easily carry, they were self-sufficient. Rufus Sage, who met many trappers in the early 1840s, explained how Mountain Men were able to survive on their own: "The mountaineer is his own manufacturer, tailor, shoemaker, and butcher; and, fully accoutered and supplied with ammunition in a good game country, he can always feed and clothe himself, and enjoy all the comforts his situation affords."[36]

DRESSING FOR THE WILD

Mountain Men were able to clothe themselves in the wild because they usually wore shirts, pants, and moccasins made from the tanned hides of deer, antelope, and other animals, material that was collectively called buckskin. Their shirts had long fringes,

This painting provides a detailed look at a Mountain Man's clothing, including his fringed buckskin shirt, fur hat, and buffalo-hide moccasins.

which were functional rather than decorative; the buckskin strands allowed water to run off the hide and the trappers could pull the fringes off and use them for various purposes, such as mending garments. In cold weather, trappers donned heavy buffalo robes and animal-skin hats, lined their moccasins with fur, and fashioned warm gloves. Although moccasins wore out more quickly than any other item of Mountain Man apparel, it was fairly easy to make a new pair of this primitive footwear by sewing together a few pieces of buffalo hide.

Even though buckskin garments were more suited for rough country and lasted longer, Mountain Men preferred clothing made from wool and other fabrics because it was more comfortable to wear than buckskin. Trappers stocked up on such items, from socks and shirts to coats made of heavy wool blankets, at the rendezvous. It took only a few months, however, for such clothing to be torn to shreds in the wild. Trappers often saved a wool or flannel shirt for a special occasion, but for most of the year they wore nothing but buckskin. Historian Bernard DeVoto explains the drawbacks of this kind of clothing: "Buckskins, though tough and so ideal for brush country, were uncomfortable. The best-smoked of them would turn [repel] rain for a good many hours [but] in the end even the best would get waterlogged and clam-

☙ A TRAPPER'S COLORFUL COSTUME ❧

Washington Irving wrote three books about the Rocky Mountains and the fur trapping business. In The Adventures of Captain Bonneville, *Irving vividly and in great detail describes how Mountain Men looked when they dressed in their best clothes for a special occasion:*

His hair suffered to attain to a great length, is carefully combed out, and either left to fall carelessly over his shoulders, or plaited neatly and tied up in otter skins, or colored [ribbons]. A hunting-shirt of ruffled calico of bright dyes, or of ornamented leather, falls to his knee; below which, curiously fashioned leggings, ornamented with strings, fringes, and a profusion of hawks' bells, reach to a costly pair of moccasins of the finest Indian fabric, richly embroidered with beads. A blanket of scarlet, or some other bright color, hangs from his shoulders, and is girt around his waist with a red sash, in which he bestows his pistols, knife, and the stem of his Indian pipe; preparations either for peace or war. His gun is lavishly decorated with brass tacks and vermilion, and provided with a fringed cover, occasionally of buckskin, ornamented here and there with a feather. His horse, the noble minister to the pride, pleasure, and profit of the mountaineer, is selected for his speed and spirit, and prancing gait, and holds a place in his estimation second only to himself. He is caparisoned [dressed] in the most dashing and fantastic style; the bridles are weightily embossed with beads [and] head, mane, and tail, are interwoven with abundance of eagles' plumes, which flutter in the wind.

my, shrink painfully, and hang baggily when dried."[37]

Before making them into clothing, trappers usually smoked animal hides over fires to make them more pliable and resistant to water. The best buckskin clothing was made from hides that had previously been used as part of a tepee, the tall, cone-shaped dwelling used by many Native Americans. Such hides had been softened by constant exposure to smoke from fires the Indians made to cook and keep warm.

WHITE INDIANS

Just as smoke darkened and cured the buckskin, the wind and sun made the skin of trappers darker and rougher. They also let their hair and beards grow because it was easier than keeping them trimmed. When more fastidious easterners met Mountain Men, their rawhide clothes and unkempt personal appearance made the city dwellers think the trappers looked like Native Americans. Some easterners mockingly referred to Mountain Men as "white Indians," though never to their face because the rough-looking men scared them. Washington Irving, however, said trappers gloried in that distinction:

> The wandering whites who mingle for any length of time with [Indians] have invariably a proneness to adopt [their customs]; but none more so than the free trappers. It is a matter of vanity and ambition with them to discard everything that may bear the stamp of civilized life, and to adopt the manners, habits, dress, gesture, and even walk of the Indian. You cannot pay a free trapper a greater compliment, than to persuade him you have mistaken him for an Indian brave; and, in truth, the counterfeit is complete.[38]

Irving was correct when he wrote that trappers walked like Indians. They had to, because wearing moccasins forced them to walk differently. People who wear shoes and boots place a heel down first and then the rest of their foot, but those who wear moccasins find it easier to put the whole foot down at once. Moccasins were much more comfortable than shoes or boots, but trapper Warren Ferris noted one drawback to the thin-soled footwear: "Prickly pear [cactus] constitutes one of the greatest evils we have to encounter in this country where moccasins are universally worn. The thorns of the prickly pear are sharp as needles, and penetrate our feet through the best of moccasins; they are extremely painful and often difficult to extract."[39]

Adopting Indian-style clothing and learning to walk like Indians were only two of the many ways in which Mountain Men copied the lifestyle of Native Americans. The trappers admired the Indians' skills, such as tracking animals and knowing how to find water in dry places, which enabled them to survive in the wild. The trappers learned these skills from friendly tribes like the Crow and Delaware, who had moved to the West and now worked alongside the Mountain Men. Former British soldier George Frederick Ruxton toured the Rocky Mountains in the early 1840s and met many Mountain Men. He was amazed by their uncanny ability to track animals by interpreting signs of their passage through the wilderness: "A turned leaf, a blade of grass pressed down, the uneasiness of the wild animals, the flight of birds, are all paragraphs to him [a Mountain Man] written in Nature's legible hand and plain language."[40]

THE FOOD THEY ATE

Mountain Men needed such skills to locate beaver and feed themselves. Their diet was limited to the wild game they could shoot, trap, or catch along with wild bird eggs and the few edible berries, roots, and plants that grew in the wild. Because trappers could carry only essentials with them, they usually had to do without coffee, bread, and other food that people back east consumed daily. Kit Carson explained how limited the trapper's daily food was: "The greater part of that time passed far from the habitations of civilized man, and [Carson had] no other food than that which I could procure with my rifle. Perhaps, once a year, I would have a meal consisting of bread, sugar, and coffee [and] would consider it a luxury."[41]

Although a diet that was mainly meat would be considered unhealthy today, trappers thrived on it. After a journey through the Rocky Mountains in 1825, William Ashley, one of the founders of the Rocky Mountain Fur Company, noted how healthy his men were:

I will remark that nothing now is actually necessary for the support of men in the wilderness than a plentiful supply of good fresh meat. It is all that our mountaineers

Mountaineers perform chores as they wait for spits of buffalo meat to roast over the campfire. Their diet consisted only of what they could hunt, gather, or obtain by trade.

ever require or even seem to wish. They prefer the meat of the buffalo to that of any other animal, and the circumstance of the uninterrupted health of these people who generally eat unreasonable quantities of meat at their meals, proves it to be the most wholesome and best adapted food to the constitution of man.[42]

To feed themselves, Mountain Men hunted deer, antelope, mountain sheep, and other animals. If there was no other meat, they ate the beaver they trapped. Sometimes they also fished in the streams. Their favorite food was buffalo, and millions of the big, lumbering, shaggy-headed beasts roamed the Great Plains and lush valleys of the Rocky Mountains. The buffalo was also the main food source for many Indian tribes. Although buffalo were not hard to find, slaying them was another matter because they were so large and tough. "No animal requires so much killing as the buffalo,"[43] said Ruxton, adding that it sometimes took more than a dozen shots to bring down a buffalo.

For F.A. Wislizenus, a St. Louis doctor who visited the Rocky Mountains in 1839, "the hunt for buffalo is one of the grandest and most interesting of which I know." In the book he wrote about his journey, Wislizenus explained that Mountain Men hunted buffalo in two ways—on foot, which entailed shooting them from a concealed spot, or on horseback, which entailed a wild ride as the buffalo fled. Either method could be dangerous. "A wounded buffalo," said Wislizenus, "attacks the hunter only when he approaches too close; but then he uses his horns as a terrible weapon."[44]

A mountaineer on horseback chases down buffalo as other members of his team fire on the animals from behind a carcass. Hunting buffalo was exceedingly dangerous.

Because an adult buffalo could weigh nearly two thousand pounds, there was so much meat that trappers usually took only the parts they liked best. The liver was considered a delicacy—they often ate it raw as soon as the animal died—as was the tongue. Mountaineers cut huge chunks from the ribs and flanks and roasted them over an open fire. The buffalo's hump, which was filled with tender, fatty meat, was another favorite. When Rufus Sage ate buffalo for the first time with Mountain Men, he was amazed at how much they loved it:

[A trapper] is never more satisfied than when he has a good supply of buffalo-beef at his command. Talk not to him of the delicacies of civilized life—of pies, puddings, soups, fricassees, roast-beef, pound-cake, and dessert—he cares for none of these things. He knows his own preference, and will tell you your boasted excellencies are not to be compared with it.[45]

After a buffalo hunt, Mountain Men sometimes preserved part of the meat for future use by drying it in the sun or smoking it. Called jerky, this meat sustained trappers when they were traveling or in periods when game was scarce.

WINTER QUARTERS

Mountain Men made most of the jerky they used during the winter months, when the cold and snow put an end to the fall trapping season. Winter comes early in the Rocky Mountains, and by early November trappers would be looking for a good place to sit out the harsh season. Some trappers went to the trading posts that were scattered around the region and a few headed south to Santa Fe, which even though it was part of Mexico had become a second center for the fur trade along with St. Louis. Most trappers, however, banded together into large groups and spent the winter in valleys in the Rocky Mountains.

When Mountain Men found a site with a good supply of water and plentiful timber, they built winter shelters, either cabins made of wood or Indian-style tepees. In the winter of 1834–35, Warren Ferris and other trappers constructed a small but snug house out of logs and wood. After completing the roof, which they covered with grass and dirt so that rain or melting snow would not seep through it, they were ready to move in for the winter. Wrote Ferris:

[We] finished and moved into our house, which was rendered extremely warm and comfortable, by having the seams filled with clay, a chimney composed of sticks and mud, windows covered with thin transparent, undressed skins, which admitted sufficient light, and yet excluded the rain and snow; and a floor constructed of hewn slabs [of wood].[46]

❧ A BRITISH SOLDIER ❧
DISCUSSES MOUNTAIN MEN

George Frederick Ruxton was a former British soldier who met many Mountain Men in the early 1840s. In Life in the Far West, *Ruxton comments on how he believes the life trappers led in the wilderness shaped their personalities. This excerpt is from an electronic version of the book on the Mountain Men and the Fur Trade Virtual Research Center Web site:*

The trappers of the Rocky Mountains [seem more like] the primitive savage than perhaps any other class of civilized man. Their lives being spent in the remote wilderness of the mountains, with no other companion than Nature herself, their habits and character assume a most singular cast of simplicity mingled with ferocity, appearing to take their coloring from the scenes and objects which surround them. Knowing no wants save those of nature, their sole care is to procure sufficient food to support life, and the necessary clothing to protect them from the rigorous climate. This with the assistance of their trusty rifles, they are generally able to effect, but sometimes at the expense of great peril and hardship. When engaged in their avocation, the natural instinct of primitive man is ever alive, for the purpose of guarding against danger and the provision of necessary food. Keen observers of nature, they rival the beasts of prey in discovering the haunts and habits of game, and in their skill and cunning in capturing it. Constantly exposed to perils of all kinds, they become callous to any feeling of danger [and] are just what uncivilized white man might be supposed to be in a brute state, depending upon his instinct for the support of life.

Trappers in the winter months had to perform many of their regular chores, such as caring for their horses and securing food. But because they did not have to spend most of the day trapping, they had time for other tasks, such as making jerky, readying their equipment for the spring hunt, and repairing or replenishing their wardrobes. In this quieter season, they also had more time to socialize. Osborne Russell remembered the good times he and other Mountain Men had while talking in tepees made of buffalo hides:

The long winter evenings were passed away by collecting in some of the most spacious lodges and entering into debates, arguments or spinning long yarns until midnight in perfect good humor and

I for one will cheerfully confess that I have derived no little benefit from the frequent arguments and debates held in what we termed The Rocky Mountain College. I doubt not but some of my comrades who considered themselves [well educated] have had some little added to their wisdom in these assemblies.[47]

Although most trappers had little formal education and many, like Jim Bridger, were illiterate, some spent their leisure hours reading whatever material they could find. Jedediah Smith, for example, read the Bible reg-ularly. For a Mountain Man, however, being religious was almost as rare as being educated and liking to read. Considered one of the most devout of all trappers, Smith once wrote to his family about his fellow Mountaineers' lack of religion: "God only knows, I feel the need of the watch & care of a Christian church—you may well Suppose that our society is of the Roughest kind. Men of good morals seldom enter into business of this kind."[48]

The crude, often brutal personalities of many Mountain Men were most noticeable at each year's rendezvous, when they celebrated raucously for several weeks during their annual

This engraving depicts Mountain Men at work skinning pelts and drying fish in a winter cabin. Mountaineers often wintered together in such cabins.

break from the daily routine of trapping. Drinking, gambling, and brawling were common features of the annual rendezvous.

MOUNTAIN MEN GO WILD

One way Mountain Men enjoyed themselves was by buying new clothes to replace their buckskins, which by now were stained and smelly. Proudly wearing new boots and wool shirts, they swapped stories with friends, drank coffee, and ate sweets and other foods that they had lacked for months.

The trappers enjoyed indulging themselves in these luxuries. But James Beckwourth, one of several African American Mountain Men, admitted that it would not take long before the trappers would start enjoying themselves in other ways:

> [It was] a general celebration. Mirth, song, dancing, shooting, trading, running, jumping, singing, racing, target-shooting, yarns, frolic, with all sort of extravagances that [trappers] or Indians could in-

---

৯ A MOUNTAIN MAN VOCABULARY ৬

The Mountain Men developed their own special names and words for things associated with their work and the life they led. The following definitions are from "A Glossary of American Mountain Men Terms" from the Web site of the American Mountain Men, a group that promotes education about this era:

AIRLINE or AS THE CROW FLIES: The shortest line between two points.

CACHE: To store something safely; also the name for the stored items.

CAYUSE: A horse as well as the name of a tribe of Indians in Oregon.

FOOFARRAW: Any fancy clothing or anything fancy on clothing.

FREE TRAPPER: A trapper who worked for himself and could sell his beaver pelts to anyone.

GONE BEAVER: A term to describe someone who has died.

GREEN HAND or GREENHORN: An inexperienced Mountain Man.

JERKY: Dried meat cut into strips about one inch wide, one-fourth inch thick, and as long as possible that could be carried and eaten on trips.

MAKE MEAT: To hunt for meat for future consumption.

OLD EPHRAIM: A grizzly bear.

PALAVER: Talk.

PLEW: Beaver pelt.

SHINING: To "shine" means to be very good at something.

WAUGH: An exclamation used by Mountain Men and Indians that usually denotes admiration or surprise. This grunt-like sound is supposed to resemble that made by a bear.

vent were freely indulged in. The unpacking of the medicine water contributed not a little to the heightening of our festivities.[49]

By "medicine water" Beckwourth meant alcohol. One contemporary observer noted that trappers drank so much that a rendezvous became "one continued scene of drunkenness, gambling, and brawling, and fighting."[50] Not having had any alcohol for months, Mountain Men went wild and imbibed as much as they could, even though alcohol was one of the most expensive items at a rendezvous—a gallon of rum cost $14.50. While drinking, they engaged in many forms of gambling, from horse racing and cards to Indian games that they played with the hundreds of Crow, Nez Percé, and Flatheads, and other Native Americans in attendance.

Some trappers spent so much money on alcohol and gambling that they barely had enough money to buy supplies for the next year of trapping. At one rendezvous, Ruxton met a penniless old man who boasted about how much money he had made and lost during his years in the Rocky Mountains:

An old trapper, a French Canadian, assured me that he had received fifteen thousand dollars for beaver during a sojourn of twenty years in the mountains. Every year he resolved in his mind to return to Canada, and, with this object, always converted his fur into cash; but a fortnight at the rendezvous always cleaned him out, and, at the end after twenty years, he had not even credit sufficient to buy a pound of [gun]powder.[51]

A TOUGH LIFE

Except for the annual rendezvous, the life of a trapper was tough. The long days were filled with hard work, and living in the wilderness denied the men a varied diet and common luxuries other people enjoyed. Peter Skene Ogden, a top official of the British Hudson's Bay Company, commented once on how difficult it was to be a Mountain Man. "This life," he said, "makes a man [old physically] in a few years, a convict at Botany Bay [a British prison colony in Australia] is a gentleman at ease compared to my trappers."[52]

CHAPTER 4

THE DANGERS MOUNTAIN MEN FACED

In the fall of 1833, members of a brigade of Rocky Mountain Fur Company trappers led by Henry Fraeb were sleeping peacefully when a thunderstorm blew through their camp. A bolt of lightning, striking the ground with a loud bang that sounded like a gunshot, killed a trapper named Guthrie. Fraeb woke up, saw the dead man, and shouted in his thick German accent, "Py gott, who did shoot Guttery?" Even though trapper Joe Meek knew what had happened, he responded humorously that the culprit was "Gawd a Mighty [God], I expect. He's a firing into camp."[53]

Meek could joke about the lightning bolt because Mountaineers faced so many dangerous situations that they became blasé about them. In his classic book *The Oregon Trail*, about pioneers heading west, Francis Parkman in 1849 wrote, "I defy the annals of chivalry to furnish the record of a life more wild and perilous than that of a Rocky Mountain trapper."[54] Parkman, who had met many Mountain Men during his own journey to the Rockies, was amazed at how they not only became accustomed to living with dangerous situations but seemed to delight in them: "There is a mysterious charm [in] danger, and few men perhaps remain long in that wild region without learning to love peril for its own sake, and to laugh carelessly in the face of death."[55]

Whether they actually enjoyed danger or not, Mountaineers encountered it daily. Grizzly bears and other wild animals could seriously wound or kill them. Some Indian tribes were always hostile to trappers, but even bands that were normally friendly sometimes attacked them. Even other Mountain Men could pose a threat: trappers working for rival fur companies sometimes stole each other's furs, and arguments even between trappers who were friends often resulted in violence. Mountain Men could freeze to death in winter cold, die of thirst in desert heat, or starve for lack of food. If they were sick or injured, there was no doctor for hundreds of miles to help them.

When danger in any of its many forms did appear, the Mountain Man often had to depend solely on himself to survive. As Warren Ferris said, trappers had to be ever-vigilant: "Every man carries here emphatically his life in his hands, and it is only by the most watchful precaution, grounded upon and guided by the observation of every unnatural appearance [in his surroundings] however slight, that he can hope to preserve it."[56]

"OLD EPHRAIM"

The one peril trappers faced daily was an attack by wild animals. The beast they most feared was the grizzly bear, whose scientific name is *Ursus horribilis* but whom trappers nicknamed "Old Ephraim" after a warlike biblical figure. Grizzlies, which can weigh more than a thousand pounds and stand over ten feet tall, were numerous in the

Mountaineers faced many dangers in their difficult life. Here, a team of trappers hurries to break camp as a prairie fire rages.

᎒ SHOOTING A GRIZZLY BEAR ᎒

Mountain Men never knew when a wild animal would attack them. In The Personal Narrative of James O. Pattie, *which details his six years as a trapper and explorer, Pattie explains how he killed a grizzly bear that was about to attack him. This excerpt is from an electronic version of his book on the Mountain Men and the Fur Trade Virtual Research Center Web site:*

On a pleasant summer evening, when nothing seemed disposed to disturb the tranquillity of our forest home, we built a fire under the cliff of a large rock, on the bank of a small creek, to roast some buffalo meat. After having cooked and eat[en] our evening repast, I was standing close to the rock, apart from the other men ten or twelve feet, all at once one of them jumped up and ran off, exclaiming "the bear, the bear!" I instantly cast my eyes to the top of the precipice, where they encountered this hideous monster seated on the rock with his mouth wide open, and his eyes sparkling like fire. My whole frame shook with agitation. I knew that to attempt to run would be certain death. My gun was standing against a tree within my reach, and after calling for the aid of my companions, I raised my rifle to my face and taking deliberate aim at the most fatal spot, fired—which brought sir Bruin to the ground.

A Mountain Man tries to fend off a grizzly bear as others rush to his aid.

Rocky Mountains. Trapper James Pattie once saw more than two hundred in a single day, and George C. Young said, "They were everywhere—upon the plains, in valleys, and on the mountains, so that I have often killed as many as five or six in one day."[57]

Mountaineers killed grizzlies not for meat but because they feared them. Many Mountain Men were killed in attacks by the big bears. Kit Carson once admitted that he was never more scared than in 1834 when two grizzlies chased him after he had killed an elk. Carson climbed a tree to safety. Because he had dropped his rifle while fleeing for his life, Carson had to stay in the tree for several uncomfortable hours until the bears left. Jedediah Smith was nearly killed by a grizzly bear who took his entire head into its mouth and nearly ripped his scalp off. The most famous grizzly incident occurred in 1823 when Hugh Glass was severely mauled. James Hall, an Englishman touring the West in 1828, described the attack in vivid detail in a letter home:

[Glass] was seized by the throat, and raised from the ground. Casting him again upon the earth, his grim adversary tore out a mouthful of the cannibal food which had excited her appetite and retired to submit the sample to her yearling cubs, which were near at hand. [Glass tried] to escape, but the bear immediately returned and seized him again at the shoulder; she also lacerated his left arm very much, and inflicted a severe wound on the back of his head.[58]

Glass was so badly hurt that two men volunteered to stay with him until he died while the other members of their party continued looking for beaver. When Glass remained alive but in a deep coma for several more days, the two men were so sure he would soon die that they left him alone, unconscious, and without weapons or food. In one of the Mountain Man era's most amazing stories, Glass survived. After regaining consciousness, the severely injured trapper somehow managed to walk and drag himself one hundred miles to Fort Kiowa, the nearest trading post.

When Glass regained his strength, he hunted down the trappers who had left him so he could get back his rifle and other possessions. One of them was a young Jim Bridger, who was scared when Glass appeared months later like a ghost from the past. Glass took pity on the frightened young man and told him, "I came back because I swore I'd put you under [kill you] but I see you're ashamed and sorry. I forgive you. You're just a kid."[59] Bridger went on to become one of the most honored Mountain Men. Glass also tracked down the second man, from whom he regained his rifle. The only reason Glass did not kill that man is that the trapper had joined the U.S. Army; Glass was afraid he would be charged with murder for killing a soldier.

OTHER DANGEROUS BEASTS

Other wild animals also endangered trappers. Buffalo sometimes gored or trampled to death Mountaineers hunting them. Packs of wolves sometimes preyed on lone trappers, and in 1833 there occurred what Joe Meek referred to as "one of those incidents of wilderness life which make the blood creep with horror."[60] Over the course of several days at that year's rendezvous, a rabid wolf bit a dozen trappers. Four of the men developed rabies and died from the disease.

Wild animals also inconvenienced trappers. Osborne Russell in 1833 had a run-in with a wolverine, an animal similar to but bigger and more dangerous than a badger. The day before Russell had shot a mountain sheep but taken only part of the meat back to his camp. When Russell returned for the rest of the meat, he found that a wolverine had consumed it. Although Russell wanted to kill the wolverine, which was still there, he did not have his rifle with him. The Massachusetts native wrote that there was nothing he could do: "The cautious thief was sitting on the snow at some distance watching my movements as if he [wanted] to aggravate me by his antic gestures. I soon got over my ill humor and gave it up that a Wolverine had fooled a Yankee."[61]

DANGER FROM RIVAL TRAPPERS

The thieves that gave trappers the most problems, however, were human. Trappers from competing fur companies often tried to sabotage each other's efforts to collect beaver. One method was to bribe Indians to harass their rivals and raid their camps. This happened in 1832 when a band of Rocky Mountain Fur Company (RMFC) trappers led by Thomas Fitzpatrick met some Crow Indians, who were usually friendly. Fitzpatrick invited them into his camp to give them some presents so they would allow his men to trap in their territory. "But before I had time for form or ceremony of any kind," Fitzpatrick said, "they robbed me and my men of everything we possessed."[62] Fitzpatrick suspected that the rival American Fur Company (AFC) had persuaded the Indians to rob his group. When beaver pelts bearing the marks of Fitzpatrick's men turned up in the possession of Kenneth McKenzie, an AFC clerk, Fitzpatrick demanded them back. McKenzie said he would return the furs "if I get my price. I make this proposal as a favor, not as a matter of right."[63] Even though McKenzie set a low price, Fitzpatrick hated buying back stolen pelts.

The rivalries between various companies were not based entirely on

With the shaft of an arrow protruding from his saddle, a mountaineer takes aim at an attacking Indian war party.

money they made from furs. American and British trappers resented each other because their nations in this era were still arguing over who should own Oregon Country, a huge area that included today's states of Oregon and Washington. The first major confrontation between British and American trappers occurred in 1825 about a hundred miles north of Salt Lake. When the two groups met, RMFC brigade leader Johnson Gardner challenged the right of Peter Skene Ogden and his British Hudson's Bay Company men to be trapping in what Gardner claimed was U.S. territory. In a letter to Hudson's Bay officials, Ogden explained what Gardner said: "[He] lost no time informing all *hands* that they were in United States Territory [and] as I had no license to trade or trap [there] to return from whence I came without loss of time. Then he replied remain at your peril, he then left me."[64] Ogden left the prime beaver area because he feared that the Americans, who outnumbered his trappers, would make good on Gardner's threat and attack if he did not. Ironically, trappers from both countries were trespassing on territory that Mexico owned.

DANGER FROM OTHER MOUNTAIN MEN

It was not only trappers from rival companies who posed a threat of violence. Mountain Men were generally rough and rowdy, accustomed to reacting physically to any situation, and they often fought each other. The cause of the fights could be something important, like who could trap certain streams, or a joking remark that a trapper believed was an insult. An example of this type of belligerence occurred at the 1835 rendezvous, when a French trapper whose name is known today only as Shunar bragged that he could easily whip any American. The challenge infuriated Kit Carson, who thought it was a slight on all Americans. Even though Carson was one of the smallest men there, he agreed to fight Shunar. The two men armed themselves and mounted horses. Carson explains what happened: "We both fired at the same time. I shot him through the arm and his ball passed by my head, cutting my hair and the powder burning my eye. During our stay in camp we had no more bother with this bully Frenchman."[65] Carson's account is from an autobiography he dictated to a journalist. However, two eyewitnesses to the fight claimed years later that Carson shot Shunar to death after wounding him. Several historical accounts also state that Carson killed Shunar because he and the Frenchman were both in love with Wannibe, an Arapaho woman Carson would later marry.

TRAPPERS AND INDIANS

The relationship between Mountain Men and Native Americans was complex. Although many Indians warred against them almost constantly, trappers and Indians sometimes became friends. This happened because they found things to admire in each other. Mountain Men envied and copied Native American wilderness skills, Indians were impressed that whites could produce fine rifles, steel knives, and other goods that the Indians could not, and each group respected the bravery and fighting ability the other showed in battle.

Some tribes allowed trappers to marry Indian women, as Carson did, and even become tribal members. Jim Beckwourth and Edward Rose were not only welcomed into the Crow tribe but became war chiefs who led Crow in battle. Beckwourth claimed he was warmly received because he had killed so many Blackfoot, the ancient enemy of the tribe that adopted him. "The Crows were highly gratified to see so many scalps taken from their old and inveterate foes,"[66] Beckwourth wrote of the grisly battle trophies he had taken.

Indeed, this intertribal rivalry had been responsible for turning the Blackfoot against American trappers. Although the tribe had traded for several decades with the British, they came to hate the Americans because of two incidents involving Manuel Lisa's Missouri Fur Company (MFC). In 1807 Lisa dispatched John Colter, a veteran of the Lewis and Clark expedition, to tell tribes he wanted to trade for furs. Colter met a band of Crow and began traveling with them. Then a group of Blackfoot attacked the Crow. Colter fought on the side of Crow, killing several Blackfoot despite being wounded himself.

It is believed that the Blackfoot were also angry that the Americans traded with other tribes. In April 1810, the Blackfoot killed two Mountain Men and stole their beaver pelts and traps. In a story that appeared in the *Louisiana Gazette* on July 26, 1810,

This painting shows a trapper in the company of an Indian. Many Mountain Men befriended Indians and even became honorary tribal members.

MFC official Pierre Menard gave this explanation for the attack:

> This adverse feeling arose from the jealousy prevalent among [Indian tribes] of those who trade with their enemies. The Crows and Blackfoot are almost continually at war. The Company detached a party to trade with the [Crows]. This gave offense to the Blackfoot who had not the same opportunity of procuring Arms [and other goods].[67]

Whatever the reason, the Blackfoot were the most consistent Indian foe Mountain Men faced. And because other tribes also warred against them at times, trappers always had to be on guard against an attack.

HOSTILITY AND CONFRONTATION

In the late 1830s, Carson claimed that hostility between the two sides was so high that "a trapper could hardly go a mile without being fired upon."[68] According to Alexander Ross, a Hudson's Bay trader (unrelated to John Astor's employee of the same name), "There is much anxiety in going through the ordinary routine of a trapper's duty and [his] gun is often in one hand, while the trap is in the other."[69] But even though Mountain Men were always on the alert, they were sometimes taken by surprise. This often proved fatal for lone men or small groups of trappers. Rufus Sage describes an Indian attack on a group of trappers: "While successfully pursuing their occupation, unsuspicious of immediate danger, they were suddenly surrounded, early one morning, by a war-party of Sioux, whose first salute was a discharge of firearms, accompanied by a shower of arrows and the sharp thunder of deafening yells."[70] This story was related to Sage by Mountain Men who happened upon the battle site and were able to deduce how the trappers had died by interpreting tracks and other physical signs of the fighting. If the trappers had had time to take cover, they might have survived even though the Sioux outnumbered them. A small group of Mountain Men, sometimes just a pair of trappers, could often keep a much larger group of Indians at bay because their Hawken rifles could kill at a greater distance than the bows and cheap guns the Indians had. When Jedediah Smith and eight others were attacked by more than four hundred Mojave, he gave his men these instructions: "Not more than three guns should be fired at one time and those only when the Shot would be certain of killing."[71] The tactic worked. So many of the Indians armed with only bows and arrows were killed that the survivors left Smith and his fellow trappers alone.

When a large party of trappers was attacked, the superiority of their arms usually decided the outcome in their fa-

Mountaineers flee after spotting hostile Indians on their trail. Indians often attacked trappers to punish them for trading with enemy tribes.

vor. This was the case in the Battle of Pierre's Hole in Idaho, the single biggest engagement ever between Indians and Mountain Men. Upon leaving the annual rendezvous in 1832, more than one hundred Mountain Men were attacked by a much larger group of Gros Ventre Indians near Pierre's Hole. The trappers, however, used their superior weapons and marksmanship to win the fierce, all-day battle. Six whites and seven Indians who fought with them died. Several were wounded, including Thomas Fitzpatrick, who in the fight earned the nickname "Broken Hand" by losing two fingers on his left hand when his rifle blew up. There are no reliable figures on how many Indians the victorious trappers killed. The Gros Ventre claim that twenty-six died, but

historians believe that the total was probably higher.

One of the most unusual confrontations came in 1808 when Colter and John Potts were captured by Blackfoot on a branch of the Missouri River known as Jefferson's Fork. After killing Potts because he attempted to flee, the Indians gave Colter a chance to live. A chief asked Colter if he was a fast runner. Referring to himself in trapper's slang, Colter modestly replied, "The Long Knife is a poor runner and not swift."[72] The chief then made Colter take off all his clothes, ordered him to start running, and gave him a brief head start before sending several hundred warriors after him.

Colter, however, was actually a fast runner. He had lied because he knew

❧ JOHN COLTER'S ESCAPE ❧

John Colter's escape from Blackfoot Indians who had captured him in 1807 is considered one of the great stories of Mountain Man survival. This account of how Colter hid from Indians is from a book John Bradbury wrote in 1819 that was included in the second volume of The American Fur Trade of the Far West *by Hiram Martin Chittenden:*

Fortunately for [Colter], a little below this place [where he killed a pursuer] there was an island, against the upper point of which a raft of drift timber, had lodged. He dived under the raft, and after several efforts, got his head above the water amongst the trunks of trees, covered over with smaller wood to the depth of several feet. Scarcely had he secured himself when the Indians arrived on the river, screeching and yelling, as Colter expressed it, "like so many devils." They were fre-

quently on the raft during the day, and were seen through the chinks by Colter, who was congratulating himself on his escape. In horrible suspense he remained until night, when hearing no more of the Indians, he dived under the raft, and swam silently down the river to a considerable distance, when he landed and traveled all night. Colter's situation was still dreadful; he was completely naked, under a burning sun; the soles of his feet were entirely filled with the thorns of the prickly pear; he was hungry, and had no means of killing game, although he saw abundance around him, and was at least seven days journey from Lisa's Fort. These were circumstances under which almost any man but an American hunter would have despaired. He arrived at the fort in seven days, having subsisted on [plants and roots].

about this deadly game that some tribes played with their captives. He escaped and seven days later showed up at Fort Manuel to tell his tale of survival.

MOUNTAIN MAN MEDICINE

By the time Colter made it to safety, his feet were cut and bleeding from the rough ground he had covered without shoes and he had numerous other injuries. Like other Mountain

Men, he had to tend to his own wounds, with perhaps a little help from another trapper. James Ohio Pattie describes what he did after being hit by two arrows in a fight with Indians:

I was assailed by a perfect shower of arrows, which I dodged for a moment, and was then struck down by an arrow in the hip. A momentary cessation of their arrows enabled me to draw out the arrow from my hip, and to commence re-loading my gun. I had partly accomplished this, when I received another arrow under my right breast, between the bone and the flesh. This gave me less pain than the other shot, and finding I could not by any effort extract the arrow, I snapped it off, and finished loading my gun.[73]

As shown by Pattie's self-surgery, the Mountain Men were tough. However, they usually had no choice but to do whatever was necessary to save their lives. In 1827 Thomas Smith amputated part of one leg below the knee after it was shattered by a lead ball in a fight with Indians. He then whittled an artificial limb so he could walk, earning for himself the nickname "Pegleg Smith" and the undying admiration of his fellow trappers.

Some surgery, however, was beyond even the rugged trappers. When Jim Bridger arrived at the 1835 rendezvous at the confluence of Horse Creek and the Green River, he had been carrying a three-inch iron arrowhead in his back for three years. Dr. Marcus Whitman, a Protestant missionary on his way to Oregon, agreed to remove it and the operation was conducted in the open with a large group of Indians and trappers cheering him on. When Whitman asked Bridger how he had been able to continue trapping with such a large object in his back, he replied jokingly, "In the mountains, doctor, meat don't spoil."[74]

The trappers sometimes became sick with fever or other illnesses. James Beckwourth once became violently ill while traveling from St. Louis to the Rocky Mountains. "My fatigue and suffering had thrown me into a fever; I became delirious, and grew rapidly worse,"[75] Beckwourth wrote. Because his companion had no medicine or medical knowledge, all he could do was give the sick trapper water and hope he would recover. After a long period of unconsciousness, Beckwourth awoke and recuperated.

HUNGER AND THIRST

Even though they usually had enough food, Mountain Men sometimes had trouble finding game. This usually happened in winter when snow made it hard for them to hunt. Zenas Leonard and other trappers nearly starved to death when a severe snowstorm trapped them in the mountains and they ran out of food. When even their horses died because of the cold and snow, the trappers decided to abandon their valuable beaver pelts and trapping equipment and walk to safety:

Provision, we had none, of any description, having eaten every thing we had that could be eat[en] with the exception of a few beaver skins. Thinking, however, that we might as well perish one place as another, and that it was the best to make an exertion to save ourselves. Each man selected two of the best beaver skins to eat as he traveled along [and we] started to try our fortune with the snow shoes.[76]

Leonard and his companions eventually found food and survived their brush with starvation. Since humans can survive much longer without food than water, however, a lack of water was a much more dangerous situation than running out of food. Jedediah Smith, who like other trappers sometimes had to cross desert regions in

An extremely resilient man, Jim Bridger worked as a trapper for three years with a three-inch arrowhead lodged in his back.

❧ MOUNTAIN MAN SURGERY ❧

When Jedediah Smith was mauled by a grizzly bear in 1823, James Clyman, a trapper in the brigade he led, sewed the wounds shut. The primitive surgery saved Smith's life but left him with prominent facial scars. In 1871, Clyman wrote about some of his experiences, including tending Smith's wounds. His account is from The Westerners *by Dee Brown:*

I asked [Smith] what was best he said one or 2 [should go] for water and if you have a needle and thread git it out and sew up my wounds around my head which was bleeding freely I got a pair of scissors and cut off his hair and then began my first Job of d[r]essing wounds upon examination I [found] the bear had taken nearly all his head in his capcious mouth close to his left eye on one side and clos[e] to his right ear on the other and laid the skull bare to near the crown of the head leaving a white streak whare his teeth passed one of his ears was torn from his head out to the outer rim[.]

after stitching all the other wounds in the best way I was capabl[e] and according to [Smith's] directions the ear being the last I told him I could do nothing for his Eare . . . you must try to stich [it] up some way or other said he then I put in my needle stiching it through and through and over and over laying the lacerated parts togather as nice as I could with my hands . . . this gave us a lisson on the charcter of the grissly Baare which we did not forget[.]

pursuit of beaver or on exploratory trips, claimed that being thirsty was much worse than being hungry: "I have at different times suffered the extremes of hunger and thirst. Hard as it is to bear for successive days the gnawings of hunger, yet it is light in comparison to the agony of burning thirst. Hunger can be endured more than twice as long as thirst."[77]

Smith knew that either condition could kill him. He accepted both hunger and thirst, however, as common dangers he might have to overcome as a trapper.

TOO MUCH DANGER

For some trappers, the many and varied perils they experienced almost daily eventually became too much to bear. One such trapper was John Colter. After being nearly killed again in a second savage encounter with the Blackfoot, Colter returned to Fort Lisa and boldly proclaimed, "I *will* leave the country day after tomorrow—and be damned if I ever come into it again."[78] Colter honored his pledge. He returned to St. Louis, married, and died three years later far from the wild lands in which he had earned his place in history.

CHAPTER 5

EXPLORING AND MAPPING NEW TERRITORY

When Jedediah Smith was growing up in Erie County, Pennsylvania, a family friend gave him a book about the historic expedition of the Corps of Discovery, which Meriwether Lewis and William Clark had led only a few years earlier. The account fired the teenage boy's imagination, making him want to travel the same unknown lands. As a trapper for the Rocky Mountain Fur Company (RMFC), Smith fulfilled his dream while becoming one of his country's greatest explorers. Smith's two most important discoveries were South Pass, a path over the Rocky Mountains that would be used by hundreds of thousands of settlers, and a land route to California. It was during the California expedition in 1826 that Smith jotted down an entry in his journal that summed up why he loved exploring new lands. On August 7, Smith wrote:

I [had a] strong inclination to visit this unexplored country and unfold those hidden resources of wealth and bring to light those wonders which I readily imagined a country so extensive might contain. I wanted to be the first to view a country on which the eyes of a white man had never gazed and to follow the course of rivers that run through a new land.[79]

Smith acknowledged that he was not the first person to view those lands, just the first white, because he knew that Native Americans had already explored every inch of the West. Like other Mountain Men, he often relied on the Indians' knowledge in his explorations. Smith notes in his journal that he hired two Mojave Indians to lead him and his party of sixteen trappers through the Mojave

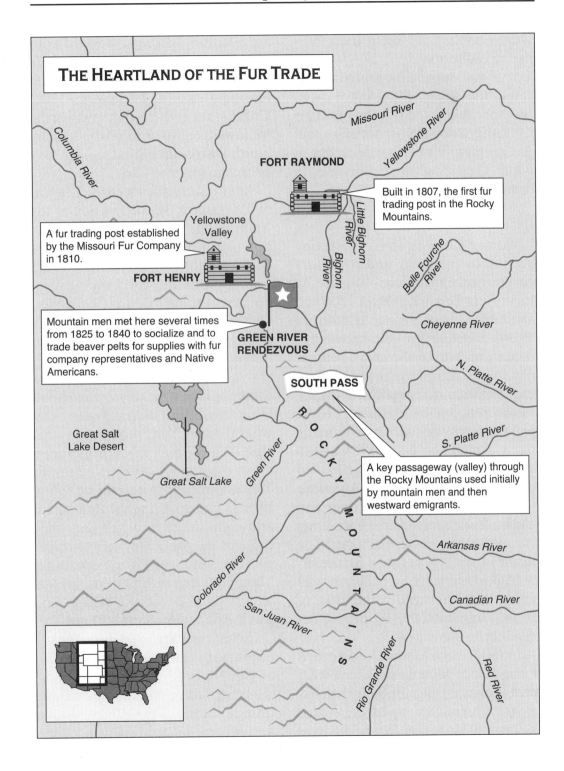

THE HEARTLAND OF THE FUR TRADE

Columbia River

Missouri River

Yellowstone River

FORT RAYMOND

Built in 1807, the first fur trading post in the Rocky Mountains.

Yellowstone Valley

A fur trading post established by the Missouri Fur Company in 1810.

FORT HENRY

Little Bighorn River

Bighorn River

Belle Fourche River

Cheyenne River

Mountain men met here several times from 1825 to 1840 to socialize and to trade beaver pelts for supplies with fur company representatives and Native Americans.

GREEN RIVER RENDEZVOUS

SOUTH PASS

N. Platte River

S. Platte River

Great Salt Lake Desert

Green River

Great Salt Lake

A key passageway (valley) through the Rocky Mountains used initially by mountain men and then westward emigrants.

R O C K Y   M O U N T A I N S

Arkansas River

Colorado River

San Juan River

Canadian River

Rio Grande River

Red River

Desert on the final leg of their journey to California.

It is not surprising that trappers sometimes needed guidance from Indians. When the trappers first arrived, they knew almost nothing about the geography of the wilderness in which they sought their fortunes in beaver pelts.

INITIAL EXPLORATIONS

Lewis and Clark explored only a tiny portion of the West, and two more government expeditions—one led by Lieutenant Zebulon Pike in 1806 and another by Major Stephen H. Long in 1819—added little to the knowledge Americans had of the area's geography. In fact, reports by the two military men created misconceptions about the region between the Mississippi River and the Rocky Mountains that made many Americans believe it was unsuited as a place to live. Pike named the Great Plains "the Great American Desert" because it seemed drier and had far fewer trees than the East. Long was even more critical, claiming, "The whole of this region seems particularly adapted as a range for buffaloes, wild goats, and other wild game. It is, of course, uninhabitable by people depending on agriculture."[80]

In 1807, when Manuel Lisa headed to the Rocky Mountains, which were then known as either the Stony Mountains or Shining Mountains, there were no maps to guide him. But he did have John Colter, who had traveled with Lewis and Clark and knew more about the area than anyone else. After leaving Lewis and Clark in 1806, Colter spent a year trapping along the Yellowstone River in what is today North Dakota and Montana. He then began working for Lisa.

After Lisa established Fort Manuel in Montana at the intersection of the Yellowstone and Bighorn rivers, he sent Colter to tell Indians in the area that he wanted to buy furs. Armed with a pistol and carrying a thirty-pound backpack filled with supplies, Colter traveled hundreds of miles in a looping figure eight as he scouted for Indian customers. On a journey that lasted several months, Colter became the first white to enter Jackson's Hole, the Wind River Valley, and what is today Yellowstone National Park. When Colter told other trappers about the natural wonders he saw in Yellowstone, such as hot, bubbling springs and geysers that shot steam and mud high into the air, they thought he was joking. Jim Bridger got the same reaction from other Mountain Men several years later after visiting Yellowstone: "They said I was the damndest liar ever lived!"[81]

Colter's solitary expedition greatly increased the knowledge trappers had of the Rocky Mountains. However, the route Lisa's men had pioneered from St. Louis to the Rocky Mountains would become even more im-

❧ THE WONDERS OF YELLOWSTONE ☙

In 1807, John Colter was the first of many Mountain Men who were amazed by the natural wonders they saw in what is today Yellowstone National Park. The first published description of the area's wildly erupting geysers, bubbling tar pits, and steaming pools of mud was written by Daniel Potts, who visited Yellowstone in 1827 with other trappers. On July 8, Potts wrote a letter to his brother in Montgomery County, Pennsylvania, in which he described what he had seen. When his letter was printed on September 27, 1827, in the Philadelphia Gazette and Daily Advertiser, *it created a sensation because of the unusual things he wrote about. This extract from his letter is from* Westward Expansion: An Eyewitness History *by Sanford Wexler:*

The Yellowstone [River] has a large fresh water lake near its head which is about one Hundred by forty miles in diameter and as clear as crystal. On the south borders of this lake is a number of hot and boiling springs, some of water and others of most beautiful fine clay and resembles that of a mush pot and throws its particles to the immense height of from twenty to thirty feet in height. The clay is white and of a pink [color] and [the] water [beneath it] appear fathomless [without any bottom] as it appears to be entirely hollow underneath. There is also a number of places where the pure [sulfur] is sent forth in abundance. One of our men Visited one of those [and] w[h]ilst taking his recreation there at an instant the earth began a tremendous trembling and he with difficulty made his escape when an explosion took place resembling that of thunder. During our stay in that quarter I heard it every day.

portant when it became part of the Oregon Trail, which an estimated half-million settlers would take west beginning in the early 1840s. The key section of this historic trail was South Pass. This famous pass was discovered by trappers not just once but twice.

DISCOVERING SOUTH PASS— TWICE

When Lewis and Clark journeyed to the Pacific coast, they crossed the Rockies at Lemhi Pass in western Montana. In their reports after they returned in 1806, they noted that the route was so steep and difficult that wagons could not use it. The Rocky Mountains would remain a giant natural barrier to west coast travel until South Pass was found a half-dozen years later.

Scottish-born Robert Stuart worked for John Jacob Astor. In June 1812, Stuart and six others left Astoria in

Oregon to travel to New York and report to Astor on his fur enterprise. Stuart and his men became lost several times trying to find a way to cross the Rocky Mountains before some friendly Crow Indians gave them directions to a gap in the mountains that at some points was twenty miles wide. On October 23, the trappers entered what became known as South Pass because the pass across the Rockies in modern-day Montana was south of the one used by Lewis and Clark.

The arrival of Stuart's group in St. Louis on April 30, 1813, caused a sensation because so few people had ever traveled overland from the west coast. Newspaper editor Joseph Charles quickly realized the importance of the pass to his country's future. In the May 8, 1813, edition of the Missouri *Gazette*, Charles explained Stuart's discovery and claimed: "By information received from these gentlemen, it appears that a journey across the continent of N.[orth] America might be performed with a wagon."[82] Despite the newspaper story the new route over the Rockies remained unknown to most trappers for more than a decade. This was because Astor kept that location secret from his fur business rivals.

In the fall of 1823, William Ashley of the Rocky Mountain Fur Company dispatched a party of eight trappers headed by Smith to find new beaver areas. Smith's party traveled across the Big Horn Mountains into the Wind River Valley, where they spent the winter with friendly Crow Indians near present-day Dubois, Wyoming. When Smith set out in February 1824, he asked the Crow how he could cross the Rockies westward into the Seedskeede, the Crow name for the Green River Valley, which reportedly had many beaver. Using piles of sand they spread on a deer hide to represent mountains, the Crow showed Smith how to get to South Pass.

Smith did not record the date on which he crossed through the historic pass to head west. But he mentioned its location to others so that South Pass would never again be a secret.

WAGONS WEST!

South Pass was the most important discovery any Mountain Man ever made. Although it gave trappers access to the Green River Valley, which includes parts of today's Wyoming, Utah, and Colorado, its significance was not the money trappers made from beaver pelts. Instead, it was historically important because it allowed Americans to settle areas beyond the Rockies.

It was not until 1830, however, that the first wagons crossed the Great Plains. William Sublette, who with Smith and David Jackson now owned the Rocky Mountain Fur Company, left St. Louis on April 10 with ten wagons loaded with merchandise for the annual rendezvous near modern-day Riverton, Wyoming. He arrived there on July 16. Although Sublette did not have to cross the mountains through South Pass to get to the rendezvous, the journey was a historic achievement. On October 29, Smith wrote Secretary of War John H. Eaton to explain the significance of the trip:

> The usual progress of wagons was from fifteen to twenty five miles per day. The country being almost all open, level, and prairie, the chief obstructions were ravines and creeks, the banks of which required cutting down. This is the first time that wagons ever went to the Rocky Mountains, and the ease and safety with which it was done prove the facility of communications [travel from coast to coast] over land with the Pacific ocean.[83]

The honor of taking the first wagons across the Rockies through South Pass belonged to Captain Benjamin Louis Bonneville, who in the spring of 1832 took a leave of absence from

Settlers crossing the plains and mountains owed a debt to Mountain Men who had previously found and mapped routes over which settlers could travel.

In 1832 Benjamin Bonneville demonstrated that wagon trains could safely cross the Rockies.

the U.S. Army to explore the West and enter the fur business. In May Bonneville brought twenty wagonloads of provisions to the annual rendezvous. On July 24 he took his wagons through South Pass into the Green River Valley to begin trapping beaver. Bonneville's feat was historic because it proved that wagons could use the pass to continue traveling westward across the continent.

EXPLORING FOR BEAVER

Smith's discovery of South Pass provided access to new areas rich with beaver. But even this promising discovery was not enough for William Ashley, who with Andrew Henry had created the RMFC. In the spring of 1825, Ashley set out to explore and locate more beaver.

On April 22, Ashley and six men started down the Green River in a buffalo-hide bull boat that was sixteen feet long and seven feet wide. The next day Ashley noted in his diary, "Our boat answers the desired purpose greatly beyond my expectation. It is Easily navigated & Carries as much again as I expected."[84] Like other Mountain Men explorers, Ashley had no idea where he was headed or what he would encounter. In the next thirty-one days, he and his men survived dangerous rapids, went hungry when they ran out of food, and often had to carry their boat and supplies long distances to bypass treacherous waterfalls.

The journey ended at the mouth of Minnie Maud Creek just north of Desolation Canyon in eastern Utah. Ashley ended his journey because he had to return to the Green River Valley for the first rendezvous, where he purchased tens of thousands of dollars' worth of beaver pelts with merchandise he and his men had previously brought to the mountains. Laden with furs, Ashley traveled by boat back to St. Louis by way of the Bighorn, Yellowstone, and Missouri rivers.

It was curiosity about another river that led Jim Bridger to discover the Great Salt Lake in 1824. When a group of RMFC trappers were idled by winter in Cache Valley on the Bear River in northeastern Utah, they began wondering where the river went. Bridger, out of curiosity, followed the river to its outlet in the Great Salt Lake. When Bridger first tasted the water, he thought the huge lake was part of the Pacific Ocean because it was salty. The next spring, however, four men in boats rowed around its shoreline and realized that it was a lake and not an ocean inlet.

HIKING TO CALIFORNIA

For Mountain Men exploring a strange new land, each discovery of a new river, valley, or lake added another piece to the geographic puzzle that the West still was to them. The addition of one piece to the emerging map of the vast wilderness often led to the location of another. The best example of this is how Bridger's finding the Great Salt Lake led to Smith's historic journey to California. After Smith became a part-owner of the RMFC in 1826, he decided to look for new beaver habitats to trap. The area west of the Great Salt Lake intrigued Smith so much that he decided to look there. "What that great and unexplored country might contain we knew not but hoped to find [areas of it] well stocked with Beaver,"[85] he wrote in his journal.

When Smith and sixteen trappers left Cache Valley in August 1826, he ventured into an area that was completely unknown to him as well as to the Indians who lived on the lake's western edge. His route took him west across Utah and into Nevada and then to the edge of the barren Mojave Desert, where the group rested for more than two weeks with Mojave Indians. When Smith learned that Spanish settlements in California were not much further west, he persuaded two Indians to guide him the rest of the way to the Mexican possession. Smith's party set out November 10, traveling through the desert and finally crossing the San Bernardino Mountains into California. When the trappers reached the Franciscan Mission at San Gabriel on November 27, they were the first Americans who had ever traveled overland to California instead of by ship.

On January 18, 1827, Smith and his men continued north through California,

❧ WASHINGTON IRVING ❧
PRAISES MOUNTAIN MEN

Author Washington Irving was greatly impressed with the bravery and fortitude displayed by Mountain Men as they explored the West. In The Adventures of Captain Bonneville, *Irving explained the qualities that helped them accomplish so much:*

It is difficult to do justice to the courage, fortitude, and perseverance of the pioneers of the fur trade, who conducted these early expeditions, and first broke their way through a wilderness where everything was calculated to deter and dismay them. They had to traverse the most dreary and desolate mountains, and barren and trackless wastes, uninhabited by man, or occasionally infested by predatory and cruel savages. They knew nothing of the country beyond the verge of their horizon, and had to gather information as they wandered. They beheld volcanic plains stretching around them, and ranges of mountains piled up to the clouds, and glistening with eternal frost: but knew nothing of their defiles, nor how they were to be penetrated or traversed.

They launched themselves in frail canoes on rivers, without knowing whither their swift currents would carry them, or what rocks and shoals and rapids they might encounter in their course.

Washington Irving discussed the heroism of Mountain Men in his works.

exploring and trapping as they went. By the first week of May they had reached the American River in northern California and were trying to cross the Sierra Mountains to get back to the Great Salt Lake. The cold and snow in the higher elevations almost killed Smith and the other trappers and they had to retreat down the mountains. While most of his men remained behind, Smith and two other trappers—Silas Gobel and Robert Evans—again challenged the Sierras. Beginning on May 20, it took them eight difficult days to cross the chain through Ebbetts Pass. When they descended they were in the Great Basin, a desert that stretched east for hundreds of miles.

Having nearly died from cold, they now began suffering from intense heat and thirst as they plodded across the harsh desert. They could only hope they were going in the right direction to get back to the Great Salt Lake. After coming close to death several times due to a lack of water, they finally arrived at their destination on June 27. Smith and his men then went on to the annual rendezvous near Sweet Lake in what is now Utah. The other trappers were stunned by their appearance. "My arrival," wrote Smith, "caused considerable bustle in camp, for myself and party had been given up as lost. A small Cannon brought up from St. Louis was loaded and fired for a salute."[86]

When Smith returned to California to bring back the rest of his men and the furs they had trapped, his journey was a disaster from start to finish. Two Indian attacks killed most of his men and Mexican authorities nearly imprisoned him because they were beginning to resent Americans, who they feared might want to someday conquer California. Smith eventually explored as far north as present-day Canada; it took him almost two years to get back to the Rocky Mountains.

EXPLORING THE SOUTHWEST

Smith's California expedition was significant because his return route across the Great Basin became a path to California for thousands of pioneers. Smith, however, was not the first Mountain Man to explore the Southwest. On June 25, 1821, a year before Ashley and Henry revitalized the fur industry in St. Louis, William Becknell placed an advertisement in the *Missouri Intelligencer* seeking "a company of men destined to go westward for the purpose of trading for Horses and Mules, and catching wild animals of every description."[87]

Becknell wanted to travel to the Southwest because Mexican citizens had recently revolted to win their freedom from Spain, which had ruled their country, and they now welcomed Americans. In September, Becknell and about twenty men left Franklin, Missouri, for Santa Fe, a Mexican possession. His route became the Santa Fe Trail, an important path for businessmen and settlers in decades to come. Becknell purchased many furs and helped establish that trade in the Southwest. In the next few years Kit Carson and scores of other trappers made Santa Fe and Taos a center of the fur trade second only to St. Louis.

As they pursued beaver, southwestern trappers explored the southern ranges of the Rocky Mountains and areas to the west. Among them was James Ohio Pattie and his father, Sylvestre, who arrived in New Mexico in 1824. Their wanderings took them to the Grand Canyon—they and other members of their party were the first white travelers to see it since Spanish explorers fifty years earlier—and in 1828 to California. In an 1831

book, James Pattie described in great detail the hardships he endured on those journeys, including attacks by grizzly bears and Indians. Pattie cautioned readers about dreams they might hold of exploring strange lands: "If there is a lesson from my wanderings, it is one that counsels the young against wandering far away [from home] to see the [far-off] habi-

A painting depicts Joseph Reddeford Walker and his Indian wife on an expedition. Walker was the first white man to enter California's Yosemite Valley.

✒ JEDEDIAH SMITH EXPLAINS HIMSELF ✒

Jedediah Smith's journeys in search of beaver from his base in the Rocky Mountains took him not only west to California but south to Mexico and north to Canada. Smith explored more unknown territory than any other Mountain Man. During these long, arduous travels to explore the West, Smith also braved more dangers and suffered more hardships than any of his fellow trappers. On December 24, 1829, just a few months before he was killed in a fight with Indians, Smith wrote a letter to his brother, excerpted here from The Westerners *by Dee Brown:*

It is that I may be able to help those who stand in need, that I face every danger—it is for this, that I traverse the Mountains covered with eternal Snow —it is for this that I pass over the Sandy Plains, in heat of summer, thirsting for water, and am well pleased if I can find a Shade, instead of water, where I may cool my overheated Body—it is for this that I go for days without eating, & am pretty well satisfied if I can gather a few roots, a few Snails. And, most of all, it is for this, that I deprive myself of the privilege of Society & the satisfaction of the Converse of my Friends!

tations, and endure the inhospitality of strangers."[88]

Another Mountain Man, however, never regretted any danger or suffering he experienced because he loved exploring. The astute observer Zenas Leonard once said of Joseph Reddeford Walker, "He was well hardened to the hardships of the wilderness . . . and to explore unknown regions was his chief delight."[89] Leonard accompanied Walker on exploratory journeys into parts of Mexico and California in 1833 in search of beaver. Walker trapped and explored the Southwest for a half-century, adding greatly to knowledge of its geography. He was the first white to see and describe the Yosemite Valley and its giant redwood trees. Walker's Pass, an easy route through the Sierra Mountains, is named after him because he was the first to use it.

Walker knew so much about the Southwest that he was hired to survey routes for the Transcontinental Railroad when it was built after the Civil War. That was just one of the ways in which knowledge of the wild areas that the Mountain Men trapped helped the nation expand its borders all the way to the Pacific Ocean.

MAPPING A NATION

When Manuel Lisa and other early explorers began traveling over the Great Plains and later into the Rocky

Mountains, they had no maps to guide them. As they wandered this immense wilderness searching for beaver, they helped fill in the blanks on maps of this unknown area by locating and often naming mountain ranges and passes, valleys, lakes, and rivers.

Although only Smith and a few other trappers had the skill to draw their own maps of the land they were exploring, many others were able to contribute what they had learned verbally. For example, in 1810 Colter moved to St. Louis after he quit trapping. He met with William Clark to provide details of what he had learned about the region's geography because Clark was making a map. Other trappers also visited Clark to share their knowledge; a few, like George Drouillard, another veteran of the Lewis and Clark expedition, even shared their own crude maps. In the next few decades, Clark used information from many sources to create the first reliable map of the Great Plains and Rocky Mountains. When Americans began heading west in the 1840s to settle the once unknown area, they were not only following in the footsteps of the Mountain Men but using maps that they had helped create.

Mountain Men also contributed to geographic knowledge of the West by reports they made to government officials. In 1825, Ashley's journey took him to areas no white had ever seen. On December 1, 1825, in a long letter to U.S. Army general Henry Atkinson, Ashley

detailed features of the region he had explored, including the rivers that had made his return trip with furs easy: "I discovered nothing remarkable in the features of the country. It affords generally a smooth way to travel over. The only very rugged part of the route is in crossing the Big Horn mountain, which is about 30 miles wide. The Yellowstone river is a beautiful river to navigate."[90]

Some of the reports made officials realize that the West was a desirable place to live. In 1835 Bonneville reported to a U.S. Senate committee some of the information that Walker and other trappers Bonneville employed had learned about the West. The report especially mentioned Oregon Country. The United States and Great Britain shared the area jointly under a diplomatic agreement, but both nations actually wanted it for their own. Noting that the Willamette in today's Oregon was "one of the most beautiful and extensive valleys in the world," Bonneville advised the senators, "If our Government ever intends taking possession of Oregon the sooner it shall be done the better."[91]

A decade later, U.S. officials would heed his advice. The government reached an agreement with Great Britain

that gave the United States most of Oregon Country, including the present-day states of Oregon and Washington. During the Mexican-American War in 1846, the United States also seized California and a huge chunk of the Southwest. Reports from Mountain Men about the area's rich natural resources and warm climate had helped convince U.S. officials that the area was valuable as a future home for Americans. After the United States acquired these new lands, settlers began moving there on trails the Mountain Men had established. It was in such ways that the Mountain Men helped their nation grow.

A JOB WELL DONE

Former British soldier George Frederick Ruxton traveled through the West and met many Mountain Men. In a book he wrote in 1847, Ruxton praised them for helping map the geography of the West:

In this highly romanticized painting, a group of pioneers, their wagons destroyed by the rugged terrain of the Rockies, continues their journey west on foot.

From the Mississippi to the mouth of the Colorado [River], from the frozen regions of the North to Mexico, the beaver-hunter has set his traps in every creek and stream. All this vast country, but for the daring enterprise of these men, would be even now a terra incognita [unknown land] to geographers, as indeed a great portion still is; but there is not an acre that has not been passed and repassed by the trappers in their perilous excursions.[92]

THE END OF AN ERA

The last Mountain Man rendezvous was held in 1840 in the Green River Valley near present-day Daniel, Wyoming. Only a handful of trappers attended the bittersweet gathering, which marked a symbolic end to their historic era in the Rocky Mountains. Even though a handful of obstinate Mountaineers would continue hunting beaver, the fur companies would quit hauling supplies to the annual gathering because there were no longer enough beaver pelts to make their venture profitable. When that last rendezvous was over, Doc Newell gave this advice to his old trapping companion Joe Meek: "Come, we are done with this life in the mountains—done with wading in beaver-dams, and freezing or starving alternately—done with Indians and Indian fighting. The fur trade is dead in the Rocky Mountains, and it is no place for us now, if ever it was."[93]

There were two factors that closed the Mountain Man era. The first was that beaver hats were no longer fashionable. As early as 1832, when he visited Paris, John Jacob Astor had foreseen the end of the market for beaver when he saw French dandies wearing a new kind of hat. "It appears that they make hats of silk in place of Beaver," Astor wrote Pierre Chouteau Jr., who ran his American Fur Company. "Beaver must go down [in price]."[94] When silk hats also became popular in America, the price of beaver pelts plummeted, falling from $6 a pound in the early 1830s to half that within a decade. Mountaineers could no longer make a decent living trapping beaver.

The second factor was that trappers had done their job so well that there were few beaver left. When F.A. Wislizenus, a doctor from St. Louis, attended the 1839 rendezvous, he noted

At the time this photograph was taken in 1864, the Mountain Men were already a dying breed.

that trappers were worried about the dwindling beaver population:

> The days of their glory seem to be past, for constant hunting has very much reduced the number of beavers. This diminution in the beaver catch made itself noticeable at this year's rendezvous in the quieter behavior of the trappers. There was little drinking of spirits, and almost no gambling. Another decade perhaps and the original trapper will have disappeared from the mountains.[95]

NEW JOBS FOR TRAPPERS

Although most trappers stayed in the region, they had to find new jobs. Some, like Joe Meek, served as law enforcement officials, while others became army scouts, gold prospectors, and guides for pioneers who began traveling across the continent to settle California and Oregon. Jim Bridger helped pioneers moving west in a different way. In 1843 he built Fort Bridger in southwest Wyoming, the first trading post west of the Mississippi River designed to help settlers complete their long journey. In a letter to a friend, Bridger explained that he was selling supplies and services to emigrants, the term for settlers: "I have established a small store [on] the road of the Emigrants on the Green River. Horses, Provisions, [and blacksmith] work brings ready Cash from them.

The same establishment trades with the Indians in the neighborhood, who have mostly a good number of Beaver amongst them.[96]

James Beckwourth also became a businessman. After moving to California, he opened a store and hotel in Beckwourth Valley and later raised cattle. Beckwourth also worked at various times as an army scout, but it was Kit Carson who became the era's most renowned scout. Carson first came to prominence in the 1840s by leading Lieutenant John Frémont on several missions to map the west. He also guided soldiers as they battled Indians and during the Mexican War and Civil War. In his later years Carson was appointed an Indian agent for several tribes and in 1866 became superintendent of Indian Affairs for Colorado Territory.

As the decades passed, however, the trappers began passing away. When Carson died on May 23, 1868, at Fort Lyon in Colorado Territory, he held the rank of brigadier general and received a military funeral. Beckwourth, who had died two years earlier while visiting Crow Indians, was honored with an Indian burial befitting his status as a former Crow chief. The body of the Mountain Man was placed on a platform in a tree. Bridger died quietly on a Missouri farm in 1881 at the age of 77.

One of the most famous Mountain Men, Jim Bridger, eventually settled in Wyoming, where he built a trading post to supply provisions to settlers.

DO NOT FORGET THEM

When the Mountain Men died, they were considered heroes by people throughout America because they had helped settle the West. Some people, however, began to worry that these legendary figures would be forgotten as the years went by. For example, Jedediah Smith was killed on May 27, 1831, in a battle with Comanche Indians. It took months for word of Smith's death to make it back east. In June 1832, a year after his death, the *Illinois Monthly Magazine* paid tribute to the trapper who had discovered South Pass and a southern overland route to California: "Though he fell under the spears of the [Indians], and his body has glutted the prairie wolf, and none can tell where his bones are bleaching, he must not be forgotten."[97]

Like the person who wrote that article long ago, historians today believe that Smith and other Mountain Men deserve to be remembered even though their era lasted only a few decades, a mere blink of the eye in the long history of the United States. The reason is that they expanded their nation's borders westward to the Pacific coast by locating the trails settlers used to move there and make it part of the United

Entitled "The Trapper's Last Shot," this late-nineteenth-century lithograph depicts a lone trapper raising his rifle to return fire as he comes under attack from a party of Indians (visible in the background).

An 1873 lithograph shows a magnificent waterfall in the region that was to become Yellowstone Park. John Colter named tar pits and thermal springs in the area after himself, as was the custom among Mountain Men.

Like the Mountain Men and other explorers, James Beckwourth was a significant contributor to America's westward expansion.

States. In fact, the trappers were being given credit for this great feat only a few years after they quit roaming the Rocky Mountains in search of beaver pelts. In 1849 Ruxton wrote this about the Mountain Men, many of whom he had met in visits to the West: "[And they] alone are the hardy pioneers who have paved the way for the settlement of the western country.[98]

In addition to the secure spot in history books they earned by helping to ensure America's westward expansion, the Mountain Men will also be remembered because they gave their names to the places they explored. John Colter lives on in the name of Colter's Hell, the tar pits and thermal springs in Yellowstone Park that he was the first white to ever see. A mountain pass, a river, and a city in Nevada are named after Kit Carson. James Beckwourth and Jim Bridger also have passes bearing their names, and scores of rivers, valleys, and communities throughout the West are helping to keep alive the names of other Mountaineers.

INTRODUCTION: MOUNTAIN MEN HELPED CREATE THE UNITED STATES

1. Quoted in George R. Brooks, ed., *The Southwest Expedition of Jedediah S. Smith: His Personal Account of the Journey to California*. Glendale, CA: Arthur H. Clark, 1977, p. 10.
2. Washington Irving, *Three Western Narratives: A Tour on the Prairies, Astoria, The Adventures of Captain Bonneville*. New York: Penguin Putnam, 2004, p. 683.
3. Quoted in Robert M. Utley, *A Life Wild and Perilous: Mountain Men and the Paths to the Pacific*. New York: Henry Holt, 1997, p. 20.
4. Quoted in John C. Ewers, ed., *Adventures of Zenas Leonard: Fur Trader*. Norman: University of Oklahoma Press, 1959, p. 94.
5. Quoted in Ewers, *Adventures of Zenas Leonard*, p. 94.

CHAPTER 1: THE FUR TRADE IN U.S. HISTORY

6. Quoted in Dee Brown, *The Westerners*. New York: Holt, Rinehart and Winston, 1974, p. 57.
7. The Mountain Men and the Fur Trade Virtual Research Center Project established by the American Mountain Men. *Life in the Rocky Mountains* by W.A. Ferris. www.roxen.xmission.com/~drudy/mtman/html/ferris/ferris.html.
8. Quoted in Robert Glass Cleland, *This Reckless Breed of Men: The Trappers and the Fur Trade of the Southwest*. New York: Alfred A. Knopf, 1950, p. 87.
9. Quoted in Page Stegner, *Winning the Wild West: The Epic Saga of the American Frontier*. New York: Free Press, 2003, p. 71.
10. Quoted in Tom Dunlay, *Kit Carson and The Indians*. Lincoln: University of Nebraska Press, 2000, p. 56.
11. Quoted in Hiram Martin Chittenden, *The American Fur Trade of the Far West*. 2 vols. Lincoln: University of Nebraska Press, 1986, 1:540.
12. Quoted in Carl P. Russell, *Firearms, Traps and Tools of the Mountain Men*. New York: Alfred A. Knopf, 1967, p. 4.
13. Quoted in Sanford Wexler, *Westward Expansion: An Eyewitness History*. New York: Facts On File, 1991, p. 53.
14. Quoted in Wexler, *Westward Expansion*, p. 55.
15. Quoted in Wexler, *Westward Expansion*, p. 56.

16. Quoted in Irving, *Three Western Narratives*, p. 33.

17. Quoted in Wexler, *Westward Expansion*, p. 59.

18. Mountain Men and the Fur Trade Virtual Research Center, *Narrative by James Clyman*. www.roxen.x mission.com/~drudy/mtman/htm l/clyman.html.

19. Quoted in Wexler, *Westward Expansion*, p. 101.

CHAPTER 2: HOW MOUNTAIN MEN TRAPPED BEAVER

20. Quoted in Chittenden, *American Fur Trade of the Far West*, 2:910.

21. Quoted in Chittenden, *American Fur Trade of the Far West*, 2:911.

22. Quoted in Irving, *Three Western Narratives*, p. 684.

23. Mountain Men and the Fur Trade Virtual Research Center, *Journal of a Trapper Or Nine Years Residence Among the Rocky Mountains Between the Years of 1834 and 1843* by Osborne Russell. www.roxen.xmission.com/ ~drudy/mtman/html/russell.html.

24. Mountain Men and the Fur Trade Virtual Research Center, *The Personal Narrative of James O. Pattie, of Kentucky* by James Ohio Pattie. www.roxen.xmission.com/~drudy /mtman/html/pattie/index.html.

25. Quoted in Mountain Men and the Fur Trade Virtual Research Center, *The River of the West* by Frances A. Fuller Victor. www.roxen.xmission.

com/~drudy/mtman/html/jmeek int/html.

26. Quoted in Irving, *Three Western Narratives*, p. 798.

27. Mountain Men and the Fur Trade Virtual Research Center, *Personal Narrative of James O. Pattie*.

28. Mountain Men and the Fur Trade Virtual Research Center, *Life in the Rocky Mountains* by W.A. Ferris.

29. Quoted in Russell, *Firearms, Traps and Tools of the Mountain Men*, p. 156.

30. Quoted in Don Berry, *A Majority of Scoundrels: An Informal History of the Rocky Mountain Fur Company*. New York: Harper & Brothers, 1961, p. 119.

CHAPTER 3: THE HARD LIFE OF A MOUNTAIN MAN

31. Mountain Men and the Fur Trade Virtual Research Center, *Narrative* by James Clyman.

32. Mountain Men and the Fur Trade Virtual Research Center, *Narrative* by James Clyman.

33. Mountain Men and the Fur Trade Virtual Research Center, *Journal of a Trapper* by Osborne Russell.

34. Quoted in Irving, *Three Western Narratives*, p. 641.

35. Mountain Men and the Fur Trade Virtual Research Center, *Life in the Rocky Mountains* by W.A. Ferris.

36. Mountain Men and the Fur Trade Virtual Research Center, *Rocky Mountain Life, or, Startling Scenes*

and *Perilous Adventures in the Far West, During an Expedition of Three Years* by Rufus Sage. www.roxen.x mission.com/~drudy/mtman/htm l/sagewntr.html.

37. Bernard DeVoto, *Across the Wide Missouri.* New York: Houghton Mifflin, 1998, p. 78.

38. Quoted in Irving, *Three Western Narratives*, p. 647

39. Mountain Men and the Fur Trade Virtual Research Center, *Life in the Rocky Mountains* by W.A. Ferris.

40. Quoted in Cleland, *This Reckless Breed of Men*, p. 30.

41. Quoted in David Roberts, *A Newer World: Kit Carson, John C. Frémont, and the Claiming of the West.* New York: Simon & Schuster, 2000, p. 63.

42. Mountain Men and the Fur Trade Virtual Research Center, *William H. Ashley's 1825 Rocky Mountain Papers.* www.roxen.xmission.com/~drudy /mtman/html/ashintro.html.

43. Quoted in DeVoto, *Across the Wide Missouri*, p. 39.

44. Mountain Men and the Fur Trade Virtual Research Center, A *Journey to the Rocky Mountains in 1839* by F.A. Wislizenus, M.D. www.roxen.x mission.com/~drudy/mtman/htm l/wislizenus/html.

45. Mountain Men and the Fur Trade Virtual Research Center, *Rocky Mountain Life* by Rufus Sage.

46. Mountain Men and the Fur Trade Virtual Research Center, *Life in the Rocky Mountains* by W.A. Ferris.

47. Mountain Men and the Fur Trade Virtual Research Center, *Journal of a Trapper* by Osborne Russell.

48. Quoted in Berry, *A Majority of Scoundrels*, p. 69.

49. James P. Beckwourth, *The Life and Adventures of James P. Beckwourth as Told to Thomas D. Bonner.* Lincoln: University of Nebraska Press, 1972, p. 107.

50. Quoted in John A. Hawgood, *America's Western Frontiers: The Exploration and Settlement of the Trans-Mississippi West.* New York: Alfred A. Knopf, 1967, p. 100.

51. Mountain Men and the Fur Trade Virtual Research Center, *Wild Life in the Rocky Mountains* by George Frederick Ruxton. www.roxen.x mission.com/~drudy/mtman/htm l/ruxton.html.

52. Quoted in Hawgood, *America's Western Frontiers*, p. 121.

CHAPTER 4: THE DANGERS MOUNTAIN MEN FACED

53. Quoted in Berry, *A Majority of Scoundrels*, p. 369.

54. Francis Parkman, *The Oregon Trail.* New York: Library Classics of the United States, 1991, p. 130.

55. Parkman, *Oregon Trail*, p. 218.

56. Mountain Men and the Fur Trade Virtual Research Center, *Life in the Rocky Mountains* by W.A. Ferris.

57. Quoted in Cleland, *This Reckless Breed of Men*, p. 44.

58. Quoted in John Myers Myers, *Pirate, Pawnee and Mountain Man: The Saga of Hugh Glass*. Boston: Little, Brown, 1963, p. 117.

59. Quoted in Winfred Blevins, *Give Your Heart to the Hawks: A Tribute to the Mountain Men*. Los Angeles: Nash, 1973, p. 44.

60. Quoted in Mountain Men and the Fur Trade Virtual Research Center, *The River of the West* by Frances A. Fuller Victor.

61. Mountain Men and the Fur Trade Virtual Research Center, *Journal of a Trapper* by Osborne Russell.

62. Quoted in Chittenden, *American Fur Trade of the Far West*, 1:301.

63. Quoted in DeVoto, *Across the Wide Missouiri*, p. 127.

64. Quoted in Cleland, *This Reckless Breed of Men*, p. 319.

65. Quoted in Dunlay, *Kit Carson and The Indians*, p. 70.

66. Beckwourth, *Life and Adventures of James P. Beckwourth*, p. 139.

67. Mountain Men and the Fur Trade Virtual Research Center, *Interview with Pierre Menard*, from *Louisiana Gazette*, Thursday, July 26th, 1810. www.roxen.xmission.com/~drudy /mtman/html/mfc/menard.html.

68. Quoted in Dunlay, *Kit Carson and The Indians*, p. 69.

69. Quoted in Stegner, *Winning the Wild West*, p. 92.

70. Mountain Men and the Fur Trade Virtual Research Center, *Rocky Mountain Life* by Rufus Sage.

71. Quoted in Berry, *A Majority of Scoundrels*, p. 175.

72. Quoted in Blevins, *Give Your Heart to the Hawks*, p. 16.

73. Mountain Men and the Fur Trade Virtual Research Center, *Personal Narrative of James O. Pattie*.

74. Quoted in DeVoto, *Across the Wide Missouri*, p. 230.

75. Beckwourth, *Life and Adventures of James P. Beckwourth*, p. 423.

76. Ewers, *Adventures of Zenas Leonard*, p. 52.

77. Quoted in Blevins, *Give Your Heart to the Hawks*, p. 153.

78. Quoted in Brown, *The Westerners*, p. 56.

Chapter 5: Exploring and Mapping New Territory

79. Quoted in Brooks, *Southwest Expedition of Jedediah S. Smith*, p. 23.

80. Quoted in Hilde Heun Kagan, ed., *The American Heritage Pictorial Atlas of United States History*. New York: American Heritage, 1966, p. 153.

81. Quoted in Hawgood, *America's Western Frontiers*, p. 119.

82. Quoted in Laton McCartney, *Across the Great Divide: Robert Stuart and the Discovery of the Oregon Trail*. New York: Free Press, 2003, p. 267.

83. Quoted in Wexler, *Westward Expansion*, p. 111.

84. Mountain Men and the Fur Trade Virtual Research Center, *William H. Ashley's 1825 Rocky Mountain Papers*.

85. Quoted in Brooks, *Southwest Expedition of Jedediah S. Smith*, p. 23.

86. Quoted in William H. Goetzmann, *Exploration and Empire: The Explorer and the Scientists in the Winning of the American West.* New York: Alfred A. Knopf, 1967, p. 135.

87. Quoted in Cleland, *This Reckless Breed of Men*, p. 128.

88. Mountain Men and the Fur Trade Virtual Research Center, *Personal Narrative of James O. Pattie.*

89. Quoted in Ewers, *Adventures of Zenas Leonard*, p. 64.

90. Mountain Men and the Fur Trade Virtual Research Center, *William H. Ashley's 1825 Rocky Mountain Papers.*

91. Quoted in Goetzmann, *Exploration and Empire*, p. 157.

92. Mountain Men and the Fur Trade Virtual Research Center, *Wild Life in the Rocky Mountains* by George Frederick Ruxton.

Epilogue: The End of an Era

93. Quoted in Utley, *A Life Wild and Perilous*, p. 176.

94. Quoted in Utley, *A Life Wild and Perilous*, p. 174.

95. Mountain Men and the Fur Trade Virtual Research Center, *Journey to the Rocky Mountains in 1839* by F.A. Wislizenus, M.D.

96. Quoted in Stegner, *Winning the Wild West*, p. 76.

97. Quoted in Brooks, *Southwest Expedition of Jebediah S. Smith*, p. 10.

98. Mountain Men and the Fur Trade Virtual Research Center, *Wild Life in the Rocky Mountains* by George Frederick Ruxton.

FOR FURTHER READING

BOOKS

John Logan Allen, *Jedediah Smith and the Mountain Men of the American West*. New York: Chelsea House, 1991. The author explains how the Mountain Men trapped beaver and helped open the West to settlers.

Gene Caesar, *King of the Mountain Men: The Life of Jim Bridger*. New York: Dutton, 1961. A biography of one of the greatest Mountain Men.

Ron Fisher et al., *Into the Wilderness*. Washington, DC: National Geographic Society, 1978. Filled with beautiful photographs of wilderness areas mentioned in the text, this book explains how the Mountain Men and others explored and then settled the West.

Andrew Glass, *Mountain Men: True Grit and Tall Tales*. New York: Doubleday, 2001. Describes the lives of the trappers and the legends that grew up around Mountain Men.

Lillian Schlissel, *Black Frontiers: A History of African American Heroes in the Old West*. New York: Simon & Schuster Books for Young Readers, 1995. This book discusses African American Mountain Men, soldiers, scouts, and farmers who helped settle the West.

Rebecca Stefoff, *The Opening of the West*. New York: Benchmark Books, 2003. This book explains the westward expansion of the United States through excerpts from letters, newspaper articles, journal entries, and other written material.

Page Stegner, *Winning the Wild West: The Epic Saga of the American Frontier*. New York: Free Press, 2003. This book has wonderful pictures, drawings, and photos and includes a lot of material on Mountain Men.

Michael V. Uschan, *Westward Expansion*. San Diego: Lucent Books, 2001. The author explains how Americans moved west, including the important part Mountain Men played in the growth of the United States.

WEB SITES

Discoverers and Explorers: Who Really Found the Oregon Trail? (www.isu.edu/~trinmich/Discoverers.html). An educational site that explains how Mountain Men helped discover the Oregon Trail.

The Mountain Men and the Fur Trade Virtual Research Center Project established by the American Mountain Men (www.roxen.xmission.com/~drudy/amm.html). This site dedicated to Mountain Men includes electronic copies of many books on the subject as well as material explaining the Mountain Man era, pictures, maps, and links to other sites.

The Mountain Men: Pathfinders of the West 1810–1860 (www.xroads.virginia.edu/~HYPER/HNS/Mtmen/home.html). The University of Virginia's American Studies Project on Henry Nash Smith's "Virgin Land" contains excellent information on the Mountain Man era.

Rocky Mountain and Plains Indian Fur Trade (www.thefurtrapper.com). This site by O.N. Eddins, author of *Mountains of Stone*, a historically accurate fictional work about Mountain Men, has solid information on the trapping era.

Wyoming Tales and Trails (www.wyomingtalesandtrails.com). This site contains a great deal of information as well as many photographs and illustrations about the Mountain Man era.

BOOKS

James P. Beckwourth, *The Life and Adventures of James P. Beckwourth as Told to Thomas D. Bonner*. Lincoln: University of Nebraska Press, 1972. Beckwourth's memoirs, dictated to Bonner, were first published in 1856.

Don Berry, *A Majority of Scoundrels: An Informal History of the Rocky Mountain Fur Company*. New York: Harper & Brothers, 1961. Berry tells the story of the Mountain Man era through the lives of the trappers.

Winfred Blevins, *Give Your Heart to the Hawks: A Tribute to the Mountain Men*. Los Angeles: Nash, 1973. An informative, sometimes lighthearted look at Mountain Men.

George R. Brooks, ed., *The Southwest Expedition of Jedediah S. Smith: His Personal Account of the Journey to California*. Glendale, CA: Arthur H. Clark, 1977. Brooks edited Smith's journal and provides additional material that makes the account more accurate and informative.

Dee Brown, *The Westerners*. New York: Holt, Rinehart and Winston, 1974. A concise look at the opening of the West, including the role of the Mountain Men in the nation's westward expansion.

Hiram Martin Chittenden, *The American Fur Trade of the Far West*. 2 vols. Lincoln: University of Nebraska Press, 1986. First published in 1902 (volume 1) and 1905 (volume 2), this set provides one of the most detailed, accurate histories of the Mountain Man era.

Robert Glass Cleland, *This Reckless Breed of Men: The Trappers and the Fur Trade of the Southwest*. New York: Alfred A. Knopf, 1950. An interesting look at the individuals who made the Mountain Man era important.

Bernard DeVoto, *Across the Wide Missouri*. New York: Houghton Mifflin, 1998. Perhaps the finest historical interpretation of the Mountain Man era ever written, this book won the Pulitzer Prize in 1947.

Tom Dunlay, *Kit Carson and The Indians*. Lincoln: University of Nebraska Press, 2000. The author focuses on Carson's relationship with Indians, whom he both battled and came to know and respect, in telling the story of his life.

John C. Ewers, ed., *Adventures of Zenas Leonard: Fur Trader*. Norman: University of Oklahoma Press, 1959. An informative, lively account of Mountain Man life by someone who worked in the fur trade.

Lewis H. Garrard, *Wah-to-Yah and the Taos Trail*. Palo Alto, CA: American West Publishing, 1968. First published in 1850, this book details the seventeen-year-old author's trip to the Rocky Mountains in 1846 and his meetings with Mountain Men.

William H. Goetzmann, *Exploration and Empire: The Explorer and the Scientist in the Winning of the American West*. New York: Alfred A. Knopf, 1967. This book includes the explorations of Mountain Men and how they helped the nation extend its borders westward.

John A. Hawgood, *America's Western Frontiers: The Exploration and Settlement of the Trans-Mississippi West*. New York: Alfred A. Knopf, 1967. A detailed look at how the nation grew west of the Mississippi River.

Washington Irving, *Three Western Narratives: A Tour on the Prairies, Astoria, The Adventures of Captain Bonneville*. New York: Penguin Putnam, 2004. The three books Irving wrote about the West, Mountain Men, and the fur trade.

Hilde Heun Kagan, ed., *The American Heritage Pictorial Atlas of United States History*. New York: American Heritage, 1966. This atlas includes detailed maps and text that explain the part that Mountain Men played in U.S. history.

David Lavender, *The Rockies*. New York: Harper & Row, 1968. This book details the history of the Rocky Mountains and includes an informative account of the Mountain Man era.

Laton McCartney, *Across the Great Divide: Robert Stuart and the Discovery of the Oregon Trail*. New York: Free Press, 2003. The book focuses on the part Stuart played in John Jacob Astor's fur company, including his epic discovery of South Pass in 1812.

John Myers Myers, *Pirate, Pawnee and Mountain Man: The Saga of Hugh Glass*. Boston: Little, Brown, 1963. An entertaining biography of the Mountain Man who became a legend by surviving a grizzly bear attack.

Gary Noy, ed., *Distant Horizon: Documents from the Nineteenth-Century American West*. Lincoln: University of Nebraska Press, 1999. A fine source book that explains history through original written documents, including many by Mountain Men.

Francis Parkman, *The Oregon Trail*. New York: Library Classics of the United States, 1991. Parkman's book on traveling the trail settlers took west includes colorful background material on Mountain Men and how they helped create the trail.

David Roberts, *A Newer World: Kit Carson, John C. Frémont, and the Claiming of the West*. New York: Simon & Schuster, 2000. The author explains how the former Mountain Man helped guide a military expedition to California.

Carl P. Russell, *Firearms, Traps and Tools of the Mountain Men*. New York: Alfred A. Knopf, 1967. An interesting look at the tools that trappers used.

Robert M. Utley, *A Life Wild and Perilous: Mountain Men and the Paths to the Pacific*. New York: Henry Holt, 1997. A well-written, informative review of how Mountain Men helped the nation expand its borders.

Stanley Vestal, *Mountain Men*. Boston: Houghton Mifflin, 1937. A well-researched look at Mountain Men and how they lived.

Sanford Wexler, *Westward Expansion: An Eyewitness History*. New York: Facts On File, 1991. A thorough look at westward expansion that focuses on the individuals who made it a reality.

INTERNET SOURCES

The American Studies Group at The University of Virginia, *Virgin Land: The American West as Symbol and Myth* by Henry Nash Smith, 1996. www.xroads. virginia.edu/~HYPER/HNS /chapter 8.html.

The Mountain Men and the Fur Trade Virtual Research Center Project established by the American Mountain Men. *Interview with Pierre Menard*, from *Louisiana Gazette*, Thursday, July 26th, 1810. www.roxen.xmission.com /~drudy/mtman/html/mfc/menard. .html.

———, *Journal of a Trapper Or Nine Years Residence Among the Rocky Mountains Between the Years of 1834 and 1843* by Osborne Russell. www.roxen.xmis sion.com/~drudy/mtman/html/rus sell. html.

———, *A Journey to the Rocky Mountains in 1839* by F.A. Wislizenus, M.D. www. roxen.xmission.com/~drudy/mtman /html/wislizenus/html.

———, *Life in the Rocky Mountains* by W.A. Ferris. www.roxen.xmission. com/~drudy/mtman/html/ferris/ ferris.html.

———, *Narrative* by James Clyman. www.roxen.xmission.com/~drudy/ mtman/html/dyman.html.

———, *Oregon: A Short History of a Long Journey from the Atlantic Ocean to the Region of the Pacific by Land* by John B. Wyeth. www.roxen.xmission. com/~drudy/mtman/html/jwyeth. html.

———, *The Personal Narrative of James O. Pattie, of Kentucky* by James Ohio Pattie. www.roxen.xmission.com/~ drudy/mtman/html/pattie/index.html.

———, *The River of the West by Frances A. Fuller Victor*. www.roxen.xmission.

com/~drudy/mtman/html/jmeekint.
html.

———, *The Rocky Mountain Letters of
Daniel T. Potts*, Letter 3. www.roxen.
xmission.com/~drudy/mtman/html
/pottsltr.html.

———, *Rocky Mountain Life, or, Startling
Scenes and Perilous Adventures in the
Far West, During an Expedition of Three
Years by Rufus Sage*. www. roxen.xmis
sion.com/~drudy/mtman/html/
sagewntr.html.

———, *Wild Life in the Rocky Mountains*
by George Frederick Ruxton. www.
roxen.xmission.com/~drudy/mtman/
html/ruxton.html.

———, *William H. Ashley's 1825 Rocky
Mountain Papers*. www.roxen.xmis
sion.com/~drudy/mtman/html/
ashintro.html.

INDEX

PICTURE CREDITS

Cover photo: David David Gallery/SuperStock, Inc.

akg-images, 11, 58

© Bettmann/CORBIS, 22, 78, 90

© Bibliotheque des Arts Decoratifs, Paris, France, Archives Charmet/www.bridgeman.co.uk, 53

© Christie's Images/CORBIS, 57

© Geoffrey Clements/CORBIS, 13, 37

© 1995–2005 Denver Public Library, Western History Collection, WHJ-10601, 43

© 1995–2005 Denver Public Library, Western History Collection, WHJ-10602, 40

© 1995–2005 Denver Public Library, Western History Collection, Z-2461, 86

© 1995–2005 Denver Public Library, Western History Collection, Z-314, 87

Hulton Archive/Getty Images, 15

© Historical Picture Archive/CORBIS, 19

Kean Collection/Hulton Archive/Getty Images, 89

Library of Congress, 18, 50, 61, 63, 65, 75, 82–83

Mary Evans Picture Library, 68

© Medford Historical Society Collection/CORBIS, 76

North Wind Picture Archives, 12, 34, 44

PhotoDisc, 32

Photos.com, 35

© Royal Geographical Society, London, UK/Bridgeman.co.uk, 46

Scala/Art Resource, NY, 88

© Stock Montage, 25

© Walters Art Museum, Baltimore, USA/www.bridgeman.co.uk, 30, 49, 80

Steve Zmina, 21, 71

ABOUT THE AUTHOR

Michael V. Uschan has written more than forty books including *The Korean War*, for which he won the 2002 Council of Wisconsin Writers Juvenile Nonfiction Award. Mr. Uschan began his career as a writer and editor with United Press International, a wire service that provides stories to newspapers, radio, and television. Journalism is sometimes called "history in a hurry." Mr. Uschan considers writing history books a natural extension of the skills he developed in his many years as a journalist. He and his wife, Barbara, reside in the Milwaukee suburb of Franklin, Wisconsin.